Single Dad Seeks: Dating Again After Divorce

Single Dad Seeks: Dating Again After Divorce

Advice and strategies on learning to find authentic love.

John McElhenney and McElhenney, John

THE PRESS OF LIGHT AND SPACE
AUSTIN, TEXAS

All Rights Reserved. Reprints upon request.

Contents

Introduction   1

Part I. Dads Are Different

1. Burn the Maps! Do You Think You Know About Dating After Divorce?   5
2. What a Single Dad Wants in the Next Relationship   9
3. Further Explorations of What a Single Dad Still Wants (Nine Months Later)   15
4. Do You Know What You Want? Dating Strategies   21
5. Dating a Single Dad - Version 2.0   25
6. A Moment of Enlightenment: The Path I'm Leaving Behind   31

Part II. Intimacy With a Dad

7. The Relationship Strategy: Moving Beyond Divorce   37
8. What I Learned About Sex: It's Almost All in Your Mind   39
9. Building the Perfect Lover: 13 Touch Points on the Path to Relationship   47
10. Sexual Power, Sexual Prime, Sexual Freedom   55
11. Our Sexual Brain and the Lies it Tells Us   59
12. Three Loves: Eros, Filial, Agape   63
13. It's Always About Time   67

14.	Seven Signs of a Healthy Post-Divorce Relationship	71

Part III. Children Come First

15.	In Relationship With a Divorced Dad: Ground Rules	79
16.	Focus on Your Kid's Strengths	85
17.	The Transcendent Single Father	87
18.	The Three Immutable Laws of Positive Co-Parenting	93

Part IV. What Dating Looks Like Today

19.	Action, Not Intention, Will Determine How Long I'm Single	99
20.	Offline Dating: Setting Intentions and Actions in Real Life	105
21.	Why Online Dating Is a Distraction and Not a Solution	111
22.	Getting Good at Blameless Breakups	115
23.	Ready or Not-Ready for a Relationship: The Dating Game	121
24.	Peaceful Easy Feeling: Looking for a Joyful Woman	125
25.	Five Myths and Five Truths About Online Dating Today	127
26.	A Sprinter in Love and How I Am Learning to Pace Myself	131
27.	Playdates for Adults: The Five Challenging Tasks of Finding a Partner	135
28.	Dating Part-Time: I Get it, it Is Hard to Make Time	139

29.	Every Other Saturday Night	143

Part V. After the First Kiss

30.	Sex Rules: The Frequency, the Fun, and the Fantasy	149
31.	Seeking, Finding, and Gifting the Spark of Love	153
32.	Here and Now: Touching Objects of Desire	157
33.	Finding Adoration	161
34.	Learning About Sex and Dating as We Go Along	163
35.	Unlocking Touch - The Love Language I Speak	167
36.	Nothing Is as Exciting as New Love, Right?	171
37.	What Men Think About Sex Versus What a Woman Thinks They Think About	177

Part VI. Sleeping Over

38.	Is it Love We're After?	187
39.	I Sing the Body Connected: Cultivating Sexual Energy	191
40.	Sexual Desire: Men & Women, the Chemistry Between Us	197
41.	Beyond the Rush of Love Is the Test of Time	201

Part VII. New Horizons

42.	Whole Adult Beings: Knowing Ourselves, Knowing What We Won't Compromise	207
43.	Love Is the Goal, Discover Your Own Path	211
44.	What's This About: Marriage?	215

45.	Learning to Love In the Present Moment	217
46.	We Have So Few Chances to Feel Loved	223
47.	Present and Future Planning in Your Relationship	229
48.	The Three Essential Elements of Love	233
49.	Fierce Love - What You're Looking for	239
50.	The Spiritual Quest for Love	241

Introduction

This dad explains it all to you. Likes, dislikes, hopes, fears. He's going to share with you his strategy for finding a "next" mate. What he wants you to know about his ex-wife and his kids. While his kids may always come first, the divorced dad needs to make room and intimacy available to a new woman if he wants to find a mate. This divorced dad knows how to express himself, and through his six years post-divorce, he's been through a lot of dates and a couple of longer-term relationships. In *Single Dad Seeks,* John tries to unravel the mysteries of online dating, relating to women, and keeping his parenting priorities straight in the chaos of love's challenges.

I

Dads Are Different

A man's divorce defines his path in life. His kids are a priority, but you need to be a priority, too. What's hard about going out with a dad? Let's explore what makes him a dad, and what things are important to consider if you want a long-term relationship with him.

1.

Burn the Maps! Do You Think You Know About Dating After Divorce?

We are all trying to figure things out. I'm working to figure myself out (wants, desires, depressions, ecstasies), to figure out my divorce (what happened, how to get over it, and how to move on in a healthy way), to figure out single parenting as a dad and, ultimately, where we find ourselves (me) today, dating and the mechanics of desire, relationship, coupling, or not coupling. And this much is clear: I have no idea what I'm talking about.

It's like trying to write about being a parent if you have never had kids. Or imagining what it will be like when you're married, before you've ever experienced it. And I believe I'm on a similar precipice. I THINK I want the next relationship. But it's only because that's what I know, that's what I think I'm comfortable with. "I'm good in relationship," I like to say to myself. I'm looking for that again.

But am I? Or is it just what's familiar? I was married the first time for seven years. Then single and sad for a couple of years and married again for eleven years. So since I was 27 years old, I've spent most of my time married. So I kinda know what that was like. Both experiences were eye-opening and transformational. And it's my natural tendency to want to get back in that couple mode again. At least I think so.

As I am embarking on this more recent path of discovering myself in dating mode, I'm not sure I have all the information or tools. I certainly don't know what my optimal date would look like, though I'm trying to construct maps. I'm doing my reading, planning, and sketching thing and trying to figure it out. But the real answer is this: there is no figuring it out.

I simply don't know. And all the blog posts and thoughts leading up to this moment, this awareness, are theoretical meanderings of a man who thinks he wants to be back in a "relationship." And they are all lies. Because I can't know. I can't imagine. I am trying to write the symphony to the next love of my life without having met her. How do I know where to begin? How can I dream her up, if she's not revealed herself to me? Quite simply, I can't.

Here's what I can do.

Pause. Relax. Enjoy the process. There is no hurry. Really. Get this. There. Is. No. Hurry.

And I can keep imagining my treasure maps, but I have to be willing to be swept away by the unknown and unexplainable. I think that's what love is. OH BOY, I used the L word. When and how does *that* come into it?

What I do know is this. Present-moment exploration is the only way to go. Present-moment conversations and discussions. Present-moment dating. Present-moment sex, if it presents itself. ANNNNDDDD STOP. That's it. Stop. Stay with the "touch" part. Stay with the conversation about current events. Stay with the fascination about the person in front of you and not the idea you have.

I do a lot of projecting. And often that projection process is misleading both to myself and the potential date. I write love poems. Occasionally those love poems are inspired by actual events in my life, a kiss, a missed opportunity, a chance meeting with an old flame. But they are no more real than my maps of the "next relationship" or finding "The ONE." Bunk. All bunk.

And yet, all very useful in self-revelation. I AM learning more about my desires. I am learning how to deconstruct my wants and desires and see which ones serve me and which ones I can leave behind. I've learned some really valuable lessons along the way, but they are not maps, they are notes.

I've learned that much of the programming I received about beauty came from pornographic magazines. But even when I was 10, I was reading *Everything You Ever Wanted to Know About Sex, but Were Afraid to Ask,* so I've been studying women and sex and pleasure for a while.

I've broken the idea, for myself, that youth is beauty. And what I've discovered is youth is more about the animal need to procreate and breed with the most attractive and available woman. And get this, women in their 20s who are uber-fit and good looking will appear to be perfect mates, to my reptilian brain. And yet, I'm not interested in procreation, or having sex with 20-year-olds or really even 30-year-olds.

I've learned that the spark comes from the eyes, the smile, and the intelligence inside. If there is joy, it usually shows through the eyes. And if there's deep intelligence, I find I'm more turned on than any physical attribute. Except of course the smile. And the joy.

I've learned that dating after divorce is different. We are much different than we were "back in the day." Our parameters and needs are very different. And our boundaries and priorities are very different as well. AND we won't put up with much bullshit before we call a foul and move on.

I've learned that the real sparks are very hard to find. And valuing that connection is often more important than any idea or roadmap I've ever made up.

Finally, I've learned that working on myself is the best strategy for finding who's "next" for me. And that includes this writing (self-examination), exercise (health and self-care), and putting myself out there as "available."

I don't like first dates, but they are a necessary evil if you are going to date. (What does that word even mean? *Date*?) And I don't like online dating. But I find it another necessary evil, like looking for a needle in a haystack. Looking for the spark to set the haystack on fire.

And really that's what I'm looking for, the fire. To feel the burn and intoxication again. This time with some tethers to the ground (and sobriety of my past experiences). But for the fire to come and burn my maps, I have to start with the spark. And since I've only seen a few sparks in the last four years, I know the journey ahead may be longer than I want. (I guess it already has been.)

And, here I will repeat myself again. I am excited and terrified about the transformation that will occur when SHE shows up. And yet I am pushing towards her, calling her in, writing love poems to HER.

I can only imagine… And for now that's all I've got. And these maps, which I will gladly set alight in her flame.

2.

What a Single Dad Wants in the Next Relationship

Let's Hook Up. Wait. I mean, Let's Go Out On A Date... We've both got some history under our belt, kids, and some requirements for what's okay and what we simply won't ever do again. (Red flags, we like to call them.) As we navigate dating again, we quickly realize the rules are very different. Our experience gives us some distinct advantages in terms of recognizing what we don't want. And perhaps our unfinished wounding might keep us from starting the dating process again.

Rules for dating a single dad

I've got two kids and a full-time job, but I'd still like to find time to be with someone.

1. Let's not rush into things.

I will admit that getting back out there, for me, as a man, initially was about sex. Today, I think sex can get in the way of learning if you like the person. And if you're going to do more than lie around in bed with this person, you might want to go easy on the seduction moves at first. Get to know if you like talking to, as well as looking at, your potential partner. I don't have any hard rules on this. But if you slow the drive to the bedroom, you might avoid getting mixed up in something purely physical. It can blur your vision when trying to figure out if you want to hang with this person for the long run.

2. I'm looking for 100% pure connection.

Half my life is behind me. I have two beautiful kids. And I'm happy with myself, just as I am. (I'd like to keep getting fitter, but my joy is genuine.) In several online dates I found myself sitting across the table from very attractive, usually younger, women who had nearly nothing in common with me. I could see myself eyeing their bodies and trying to imagine the sex, but I stopped myself, pretty quickly, even with the fantasizing. It takes a lot to get to a second date with me. Today, I'm even getting pretty stingy with first dates. I don't want a "date." I don't want nice. I want my next relationship to start out with the potential to go the long distance. I've never been a casual dater.

3. I'm into moms.

If my date doesn't have kids, she probably won't have much in common with me. At our age, kids are either a choice you made or one you didn't. And nothing against the non-parents in the group, but I'm so wrapped up with my kids that if you don't have that same passion and joy, we're probably going to have to look for things to have engaging conversations about. If you have kids, we've got an immediate starting point for everything. Trying to talk about your kids with a woman who's not a mom… Well, they just don't get it.

4. Let's be clear about this.

Games of any kind are an immediate time out. Passive aggressive might have worked in some other decade, but as adults, we should've gotten that silliness out of the way. One thing I will tell a first date, "You can ask me anything. In fact, I prefer the hard questions. I'm trying to learn the answers myself. I will always try to answer honestly." The first relationship I've had since my divorce went right for it. We went through the whole process, getting to know each other, dating, breaking up, without any drama. None. We're still friends. That's how it needs to be. Let's do without all the crazy stuff.

5. Brutally honest

If it's not a fit on the first date, I'm going to try to let you know gently and quickly that it wasn't a fit. I think initial attraction is something we can't really control or completely predict, but I also don't think we can do without it.

I have created a dog metaphor to help me explain what I'm talking about. And I usually share this concept on the first date. (Hmm. Maybe this explains a lack of second dates.) Here it is. Two dogs meet up in a park. One of three things happens: both tails are wagging, one tail is wagging, or neither tail is wagging. It's as simple as that. I was born with a Boston terrier's body. I can be several different sizes of Boston terrier, but if you're into whippets and poodles, we're probably never going to be a match. And there's no accounting for taste. I think some of this is hardwired.

6. The spark is only a start.

If the chemistry (tail wag) is ON, there are still a ton of steps along the path before we're in a relationship. We need to have intellectual compatibility. (If I'm a reader and you're a reality TV junkie, we might not go the distance.) We need to synchronize our schedules over time. Kids, work, and all the other stuff we're just remembering we love to do have to be the priority. It may take several months to get in our first four dates, but... Like I said earlier, we shouldn't be in a hurry. And then we've got all the negotiations about how and when we want to see each other. (Let's not start with jumping in bed or looking at vacation calendars for a while. Okay?)

7. Fearless commitment to monogamy

At first, divorce may seem like we've gotten the key to the kingdom of sex again. It's not that easy. If that IS what you are looking for, go for it. I won't be in your queue. If we do decide to sleep together, I want to know that we've just become mutually exclusive. That might be a stretch if you're playing the field or not sure about what you want. It's not difficult for me. By the time we get past first base, I'm letting you know that I am into you. And if you want to go further, we've got to establish some mutual objectives. (If we're about to sleep together, I can assure you we've had this conversation.)

8. Feeling the feelings

Men are often accused of not feeling their feelings. Feelings can be scary for both men and women. But as we begin navigating our time together, we've got to be able to talk about whatever we're feeling. The beauty of that is feelings include the ability to fully love. So when opportunity arises, I look forward to being 100% present with my feelings. There might have been a disconnect on those terms in my previous marriage. But I'm a learning individual. I know that I feel deeply, and I enjoy being expressive of those feelings. If feelings scare you, that might be something for you to look at. Feelings are the key to compatibility, in my opinion.

9. Dating women my age

Yes, I selected some potential younger dates and knew their age and also that they had not had children. I learned as a result of these mistakes. It's pretty telling for both men and women when their profile says they are 50 and they want to date partners who are 30-40. I'm not that guy. I'm pretty clear about wanting a woman who's experienced a lot of the world. And in that model they've probably had kids and are generally within five years of my age, on either side. My first girlfriend post-divorce was a couple of years older.

10. Who pays, who is the predator, and who's demanding sex?

Many things are wrong in the relationships between men and women. I am not an apologist for the cultural norms that have stacked the deck against those of us who are trying to elevate the discussion about it all. And I think our culture's focus on youth is way off base. Someone commented on my blog that porn was to blame, but

I'm not sure porn is any more the driver then the Miley-Cyrus-type circus of celebrity and mainstream media. Our culture feeds on extremism. And it has an effect on all of us, adults and teenagers.

The discussion I am hoping to facilitate is the antithesis of these issues. That's why I am trying to come out with my individual perspective that seems to be different from the experiences you've had. We learn. We evolve. Or we don't. I am hoping to get better, clearer, and more honest with each attempt at being in a relationship. We (men and women) need to have more frank discussions about desire, sexual preferences, and how we want to relate to each other in and out of the bedroom.

I look forward to having another opportunity to learn about myself "in relationship" at some point. I'm happy and patient right where I am. But I believe by having my priorities clear and articulated, I can do a better job of finding and sorting through the process of finding that NEXT RELATIONSHIP. I wait enthusiastically.

3.

Further Explorations of What a Single Dad Still Wants (Nine Months Later)

Don't kill the heat by worrying about the fire damage.

One of the things I've learned thus far is never assume you have it figured out. This list has come back to bite me on more than one occasion. Sure, I'm okay with being a single-parent blogger and getting into the dating/relationship space, just a bit. And I'm okay with telling you I write about stuff, and I might even write about our relationship, should we hit it off.

Well, let me tell you how my last three months have gone. We hit it off, sort of. We hit some parts of relating in spades and other parts, not so much. Here are a few more points that I've learned in the course of dating another single parent for three-plus months.

1. Long-term relationship or bust

Saying that I'm only interested in a long-term relationship, or marriage, is not very accurate. This was the first issue that freaked this woman out. She politely said, "We've got a lot of heat, but I don't think I want the same things you want. I'm not looking to get married again. Ever. So if that's your goal, you'd best keep looking."

But…

There was no argument. However, we were both sad when our chemistry and joy were absent again from our lives. She texted later, "do you want to hit." We were tennis buddies. And what unfolded from that "date" was an agreement that we would stay in the present and not get too far ahead of ourselves. Starting a relationship and having a Relationship are two different things. Couldn't we just enjoy our present moment together? Sure, let's try that.

I have had to recant my declaration of long-term quite a number of times. I know what I want is a long-term relationship. Not a question for me. The question is, what does that look like? That's the sticky wicket.

2. If you stay present, you won't get scared.

It's the future that gives my friend the freak-out posture. The best case scenario, even in her mind, is a bit diffuse. And it is also pretty abstract when I start thinking about next year, or two years from now. I'd like to still be involved with this highly intelligent woman, whom I completely dig on all burners, but who knows… Right. Who knows? Certainly we don't know. We're just starting out. But that's our pattern and our fear that comes into our minds when we start mapping out too far in advance. And, in all fairness, it's not necessary. NOW is it. Stop with the "what if."

3. Making it up as we go along

So we don't really have a word for what we "are." I don't like dating, so I'm not dating her. She doesn't like the idea of a long-term relationship, so we're not doing that either. Do we need an easy handle on what we are forming between us? No. Is it more convenient if you are able to say "my boyfriend" and "my girlfriend"? Maybe a tad better than my lover or my life-mate. But please, we're splitting hairs. Do we like to be together? Yes. Are there things we like to do together besides fool around in bed? Yes. Then do that. Do all of that.

4. Hold on loosely.

So she doesn't want to read my love poems. She doesn't need to read my blog. I don't have to get my yayas by getting her to tell me I'm a good writer or a swell poet. I don't need that reassurance. I'm okay with who and how I am. And she also doesn't want to hear if I'm still looking for the next relationship, though she wants to be clear that she's not it. Well, sometimes she's okay with that. We're figuring that out, too. What we are, what we will be. Who knows? If I think I know, I'm delusional. I have no idea. What I do know is we have an honest relationship. She's able to say when she's pissed off at something I've done or written. And I'm able to let her breakup demands roll off my shell until we're able to meet in person and talk things out. That's as far as we've gotten. And that's fine.

5. Texting is dangerous and lovely.

The minute there is a misunderstanding on text, stop trying to figure it out or argue it out on text. STOP. Get face-to-face and talk. You cannot read the person's attitude. You have no idea what is really going on when the text comes across saying, "I've gotten some very disturbing news." Um, what? Just STOP. Trying to answer complaints, answer requests for reassurance, basically answering anything that has an edge to it, is very risky to continue via text. Our average is 1-out-of-10. Just forget about it and ask for a meeting. "Sweetie, let's get together and talk about this." That's all you need to know.

6. The first three months are not real.

We're still pushing boundaries, still finding rhythms, still managing two single-parenting schedules to try to find time to be together. The good thing is we ARE trying to get together. We're both trying. We both make efforts. And that's enough for now. Just as the long-distance relationship has a tendency to create a honeymoon extension, the single-parent dating cycle is quite gated by our ability to find the time to be together. That's probably a good thing.

7. All about the kids

In the end, our kids come first. We've got to make them the priority. They are dependant on us and our availability. Our adult relationships are not. Your "dating" needs to be able to weather some disappointments. When the kid is sick and the date doesn't go off as planned, it's got to be okay. And that goes back to the idea of single parents dating other single parents. We get it. If at some point in the future we decide to blend our family lives more, we'll have more insight into the inner workings of the other parent-child relationship. Until then, we should butt out off all things kid related. Other than giving their kid priority access to them, obviously.

8. I have no idea.

Where are we going? Why should I really be concerned about not knowing what the future holds in store for me and my special friend? There are over a hundred things that could upset the apple cart in the next three months. Why spend energy and time trying to figure the future out? Don't. Go read some *Power of Now* (by Eckhart Tolle). Go for a walk alone when your new partner can't make it. In the end, go on about your lives **as if...**

As if the other person is just a "nice to have" and not a "must have." Going that far and putting too many expectations on the future of your relationship are enough pressure to blow it up right there. Don't kill the heat by worrying about the fire damage.

4.

Do You Know What You Want? Dating Strategies

Figuring out what went wrong in your marriage is a big puzzle. I hope you've done some work on your issues before you start looking for your next relationship. We're going to start with the premise that you've solved some of your own issues and identified some of the things that split you apart.

Online dating

While I do think there is value in online dating, I also believe problems are inherent in the social click-me culture. But let's look at what's great about online dating.

> 1. Browse the available field from the comfort of your home.
>
> 2. Put your personal value proposition together (what you have to offer).
>
> 3. Put your wants, desires, and dreams out there (what you are looking for).
>
> 4. Put what you like to do out there. (On Friday nights enjoying being on the couch or in a night club are two very different trajectories.)
>
> 5. It helps you get your image together. (You didn't

post that one you took in the bathroom, right?)

6. You can learn what parts of your profile people are picking up on. Because you'll ask them on the date.

7. Try some dates. Learn what you like and don't like about dating.

8. Low commitment of time is required to get a date lined up.

9. Flirting online is fun.

10. Seeing all the potentials is inspiring.

Offline dating

The goal of online dating is to get to an offline date. Meeting in person is the only way to see if there is chemistry going both ways. Photos are interesting, but they lie. Profiles are interesting, but they are about 50% made up. You've got to go toe-to-toe, face-to-face to understand if you want to date this person.

I found that my efforts online were fun and semi-fruitful (my first relationship after divorce was from Match.com), but they were lacking in the more fundamental aspects of relationships.

1. Do they like to do the things you like to do? (Not just say they do.)

2. Does your heart race when you are near them?

3. Can you pick up the returning vibe when you are with them?

Being with someone should be an energetic experience. Both of you should feel energized after being together. And you can't find that through text messages or emails. And you can't really see what a person looks like from photos. You get their BEST SIDE, but you want ALL SIDES.

Priorities

This is the biggest decision for you to make. What are your must-haves and what are your deal-breakers? And know this, these things will change. Things you thought were must-haves might fall off the list when you meet the right person. A few of my priorities looked like this:

- Must love being active
- Has a positive personality
- Whip smart
- Athletic body shape
- Funny
- A single mom

Then know that your priority list is changeable and re-sortable. And you may change it frequently.

A road map

All of your ideas for the person you are looking for are more like ancient treasure maps than today's GPS-accurate maps. You do need a map, however. This book represents mine.

And then you have to know this. Your map will be burned and charred from adventures. This is not a bad thing, it's part of the process. Your map is an idea of where you want to go.

When the right person shows up, all of your priorities and maps will be blown away. At least that's what you hope for. You need the maps and plans and strategies. But when the right person shows up, you will be amazed how little those things mean.

Get your plan. Try online if you want. Get to offline. And then see what fits and what doesn't. You need someone who's willing to fight for the relationship. When you both played that role in your last relationship, you might have found a like-spirited person who will fight for your love, just like you will fight for theirs.

That's my dream, and I'm sticking to it.

5.

Dating a Single Dad - Version 2.0

Let's re-examine my requests from my first *next* relationship list and see what has changed.

My Initial rules for dating a single dad

1. Let's not rush into things.

2. I'm looking for 100% pure connection.

3. I'm into moms.

4. Let's be clear about this.

5. Brutally honest

6. The spark is only a start.

7. Fearless commitment to monogamy

8. Feeling the feelings

9. Dating women my age

10. Who pays, who is the predator, and who's demanding sex?

Rushing, connection, and honest

Why rush the moment? You're only going to be in the first moments of your relationship once. Chill. Enjoy the thrill, the chase, the capture. For me, kissing is a big deal. I don't kiss on the first date unless there's something remarkable happening. And even then, it might be more of a hug and a peck and not a full-blown French kiss.

Go slow initially. Make sure your emotional and mental state is solid. Then, when the right partner arrives, be prepared to have all your rules, lists, and ideas torn to shreds with the passion of your connection. When you feel that love, every circuit in your body goes from resistance to acceleration. If it's not a map-burning connection, you should even give that time, as connections do grow hotter over time.

Moms... or not

Initially I figured only another single parent would understand the occasional "dad's checked out, attending to his kids" moment. But that's not necessarily the case. My third relationship post-divorce was with someone who never had kids. Although I didn't think she ever would love my kids the same way she loved me, she was 100% supportive of my relationships with them. Their mom, not so much, but that's water under the bridge. So scratch that requirement off my list.

The spark and monogamy

You gotta have the spark. That's the key ingredient for pulling my heart-strings. Yes, I'm sure chemistry of some sort develops over time, but I'm pretty convinced that the YES-VIBE is what kept me connected to my previous wife even when things were going south. I was so "into" her that she could do a lot of crappy stuff before I got mad. If the spark is not there, I think monogamy might be a bit more of a challenge. I've never cheated, but I have only committed to relationships that had the spark first.

Feelings

You've got to be able to express them to each other. She's GOT to be able to get mad at me so we can work through what's upsetting her. I've got to be able to show her my vulnerability so that she can respond and reply in ways that support me. In my most recent relationship, we were lucky to have so many YES connections right off the bat. THEN when my depression kicked in, full-bore, as bad as anything I experienced while married to the mother of my kids, even then she was prepared to stick it out with me.

Sex and dating

Sex is amazing. Sex is meant to be amazing. Don't give your amazing to too many people, it can result in a lot of confusion for both you and your partners. I tried casual sex once. It was fun for two times, and then it sucked. When I commit to having sex with someone, I'm opening myself up to a relationship with that person. Sex without that connection is more like masturbation. It's fine, and yes, it's better with someone else, but not all that much better.

When I have sex with a woman I am saying, "You're the one. I don't want to, and won't, have sex with anyone else." It's that commitment on my part that keeps it real and that keeps me from getting into uncomfortable situations when the dating shows up some real issues. Keep it in your pants until you KNOW this is a long-term thing. Short-term sex is unappealing to me. That's what porn is for. With a real, live human being I want to be 100%

present and honest, and I can't do that if I'm only thinking about sex.

Dating and money

I once dated a woman who made three times the money I made. We still split the checks. Here are my simple ideas about "who pays."

- Both people should offer to pay. ("We can split this.")
- It's okay for the man to pay as part of the dating plan as long as that's okay with the woman. If the woman wants to pay, to make it equal, then that's what you should do.
- If money is an issue and your date wants to go to a really expensive place or drink expensive wines (as in the case of 3X woman), then you have to say something. Getting overdrawn on your debit card is not pretty and not fun. Most of all, it's not honest or necessary. If she's got a lot more money, let her know she's going to have to float some of her expenses.

Summary

Go for 100%. Don't settle for an almost relationship because you are lonely. That's the time you need to take more interest in yourself and what you are doing to become a more attractive and delicious partner. If it's not working out, don't go further or go on more dates to "make sure." If you're not feeling the spark, it's probably not going to arrive on Date 2 or Date 3.

If you are feeling the lack of any chemistry, it's okay to bail on the date. Don't extend the conversation to a second cup of coffee or glass of wine if these are merely pleasant. The other person might be picking up your vibe, but if you are NOT, then don't prolong the miss. At the end of a "meh" date, don't pretend you're going to call each other. Just say, "Thanks, I enjoyed it."

You deserve a kick ass relationship. You deserve honesty, monogamy, and awesome sex. Make sure you're not settling for Mr./Mrs. Meh. In the long run, only the magic will preserve your relationship, so you'd better get on with the task of finding THE ONE.

6.

A Moment of Enlightenment: The Path I'm Leaving Behind

I could hope for an Age of Enlightenment, but I'm being realistic.

I can comfortably say that I have passed through the Dark Ages, and I am somewhere in the Between Ages. But I also have reached a moment, this moment, where I can see certain things quite clearly. Although the path ahead is not clear, the mistakes of the ages behind have never been clearer.

The other day I was describing what I was seeking in my relationship. "Someone who is warm and deep feeling." You see, I believe those are two of my strongest qualities.

> 1. Warmth: expresses joy and togetherness easily, often encourages and brings energy and happiness into a room on arrival.
>
> 2. Deep feeling: able to connect with the emotions that are often the cause of suffering, disappointment, and immense joy.

It is my understanding, at this moment, that deep feeling and warmth are the two qualities I did not hold out for in my first attempts at marriage. There are a lot of traits to connect and disconnect with people on, and somehow my other "needs" or "connective traits" seemed more important at the time. Maybe I was lonely. Maybe I lost sight of what was possible. But somehow I "settled" regarding these two qualities in both my previous marriages.

My most recent wife was beautiful, smart, devoted, and organized. Yet the labels of "warmth" and "deep feeling" are probably not going to be generally applied to her personality. That's okay. We are all different. And maybe what is warmth to me is something different to others. That's all fine. But for me, even at the beginning, when we were courting madly, that spark of joy was missing. The deep feeling seemed to arise when we were engaged in lovemaking and enjoying a glass of wine, but of course, you can't always be fking and drinking, there's a lot more to life.

So outside of those kinds of extraordinary circumstances, what is the quality of the person you are looking to be with? When the tasks become more mundane, what is the timbre of the relationship?

So this momentary illumination of these two critical traits is important. I don't have to try and convince myself that these two traits are more important than a flat stomach or an activated and creative imagination. Both of my wives had brilliant creative impulses, and both were beautiful to look at.

Online dating is an opportunity to refine your perspective. In many ways, building a profile on an online dating site is like setting intentions.

> 1. We have to say who we are. Here is what I want you to know about me. Here is how I present myself in my best light. Here is a picture that I think makes me look cuter than others.
>
> 2. We have to begin the process of identifying the

person we want to be with next. Initially it's a bit like browsing for a house online; you are looking for the initial curb appeal. Again, these photos are some of the best this woman could find to represent who she wants you to see. Photos lie.

As we travel through this process, appraising, arranging, asking, flirting, explaining… we get a chance to refine our pitch and our wish list. And once we get clarity on those non-negotiable traits that we must have in our next relationship, the task is much easier. Or, at least, clearer.

Now I have it. **At this very moment I believe that everything comes after my two main criteria: warmth and deep feeling.** Of course, without curb appeal, I won't even have a chance to say hello. (This cuts both ways.) And I believe my "enlightenment" comes from the realization that other traits are important (1. intelligence, 2. outward beauty, 3. self-awareness/spirituality), but without **warmth** and the **ability to express it at a deep level**, well, without that we have the path I am leaving behind.

11

Intimacy With a Dad

He's had kids, so that's not really the point any more. What does a dad need out of intimacy? How can a divorced dad provide comfort and ease in different ways? You've only got him every other weekend, so how can you make the most of your time with a divorced dad?

7.

The Relationship Strategy: Moving Beyond Divorce

I'm kinda tired of writing about the ex-y. I'd like to start the new chapter, the new symphony.

One day, as I was waiting for one of the "women with potential" to show up, I wrote this Relationship Strategy list. Just like I would for an online marketing project I was taking on. Here I was, getting ready to hang out with this woman, and I'm designing the strategy for getting beyond dating and into a relationship. I knew this wasn't really just about her; it was a framework that I was hoping would be trashed by passionate overtures. Um, I'm still waiting.

Here's my strategy:

1. Establish mutual connection.

2. Spend time together.

3. Learn + listen.

4. Experience life.

5. Be yourselves.

6. How does it feel?

7. Learn each other's relating style.

8. Define love language.

9. All good? Add kissing if you want to.

10. Kissing may lead to lovemaking.

That's it. Pretty simple. The part that's not simple is negotiating and navigating the process with someone who is terrified of moving down the list. Or maybe inexperienced at deep relating.

A question I am asking myself in regards to the woman who is at least present is, "Can the crazy unbridled passion still be unlocked when kissing comes into play?" Because if it's all cerebral and calm and calculated, I'm concerned she might not ever light up.

But I am committed to seeing this woman <u>off the planet of overthinking</u> and into something. I'm not sure it will be kissing me, but hey... I'm still interested.

The second "woman with potential" went missing. We exchanged messages and a few potential schedules, and she chilled them each time. I'm not surprised, as she seemed to have a much more complete life. I was about to ask her about "holding on loosely, versus pursuit." I have the feeling she prefers to be in complete control. And again, if I fit in, great. If not, she didn't really NEED a relationship in the first place.

Are adults often stuck in this model of relating? I love the idea of independence; I'm just understanding the value and risk of giving up my solitude and creative time. But it's not where I want to end up. I aspire to be in a connected relationship. And part of that connectedness is having a partner who wants to be deeply connected as well.

8.

What I Learned About Sex: It's Almost All in Your Mind

The mind is the most powerful sex organ of all.

I'm a very sensual and sexual person. In Gary Chapman's book, *The 5 Love Languages,* my picture represents the touch-centered person. So when my sexual interest and prowess began to wane in my early 50s, I got a little concerned. I mean, I had never needed any help catching an erection, and all at once I was having a problem even with an eager and willing partner. So I started doing some reading.

As my erectile non-cooperation began, I started looking for answers. I wasn't sure if it was my age, my mental state (I was a bit depressed), or the woman I was with. I was flat-out confused. Several factors that I was clearly aware of were at play.

> 1. I was recently divorced.
>
> 2. I was depressed.
>
> 3. I had started some SSRI medication to help with the depression.
>
> 4. I was in the first relationship since my divorce, and my partner was enthusiastic and joyful.

ANNNND, I couldn't get a hard-on on demand. WTF? Or should I say, WT(no)F. These are the first few things I learned:

> 1. A good portion of sex is in my own mind.
>
> 2. SSRIs have a huge incidence of sexual side effects. (More on the second level of this issue, in a bit.)
>
> 3. A sexually aware partner is equally into getting themselves off as getting you off. When you can't perform, your partner might begin to doubt her attractiveness to you or even question the relationship.
>
> 4. My issue was not erectile dysfunction, and I was not in need of the little blue dick helpers.

But a longer period of exploration and education was needed in order to get me in the position I am today. (Happy, well fkd, and joyfully engaged with or without erection and orgasm). As I moved through this first sexual-and-engaged relationship, I passed through several phases.

Relationship Phase 1: I'm depressed. I have no idea what I like. I don't even crave ice cream. So, I don't desire her, it's probably just the blues talking. (This was the first month.)

Relationship Phase 2: Okay, it's not all me. I can learn to love her, to be into her, and my mind is the key. (This was the second month.) I started reading *Sexual Intelligence* by Marty Klein and really giving some thought to my situation, both to myself and to this lovely woman, who really liked me.

Relationship Phase 3: Well, perhaps I'm just not that into her. Sometimes that happens. There was a chemistry mismatch. Nobody's fault. I developed my Dog Rule of Dating from this point. But I began to explore the idea of not being in this relationship (the third month.)

We had an amazing discussion the morning after I broke it off. We had breakfast at a Denny's. Sitting across from her I realized how much I loved her. I loved her, but I wasn't sexually aroused by her. It wasn't porn, or unreal youthful ambitions, or some other disconnect. It was simply a mediocre response sexually to my reptilian brain. I wanted a greyhound and she was a fancy poodle. (My apologies to her for the analogy.)

Moving on

The next relationship I had was highly sexual. In fact, the sex was about all we had. She would have knee-jerk reactions every few weeks, just as we were getting close, and break up with me. All my doubts of sexual dysfunction on my part evaporated with this lovely and intelligent woman, who was not ready for a relationship, much less a relationship with me. We didn't last very long, but long enough to show me that sex is not everything. In fact, our sexual chemistry got in the way of me seeing early on that she was not right for me. So we screwed our way into the summer before the fifth breakup finally broke through my sexual-fueled denial.

And onward through the fog of single dadhood

So in the first relationship I learned about TOUCH (I had never experienced someone so touch-centric), and I knew I would never put up with anything less. In the second relationship I learned that SEX could be awesome, but the relationship could be super bad. And that set up my quest for the next love of my life.

Goal: Touch + Good Sex + Emotional Intelligence

When this woman showed up, I was overwhelmed with the passion and connection we experienced from the first kiss. We both stripped away our inhibitions and hesitation in the heat of our connection: intellectual, sexual, spiritual. Sure, there were things we needed to work through, but this woman was on a different level altogether. So many things were ON that I was really dismayed when my mental state collapsed under the stress of a new job, new house, ANNNND new girlfriend.

That's when things got really interesting. Given every opportunity to run away, declare me a perfect mess, she didn't run away at all. She stepped in, stepped up, and engaged with me on all levels. I don't know how she did it. I don't know if it was the chemistry and amazing connection we had in the first 45 days, or if she had already fallen in love with me, but I can tell you that I was feeling totally unworthy and unlovable. And yet SHE LOVED ME ANYWAY.

Then the issues with my sexuality returned in spades. Yes, a new round of SSRIs was inserted to cut off my looming fall into depression. And YES, the Lexapro generic created a new set of problems that I had not experienced before. The depression was also interfering with my ability to focus or stay focused on sex. Even while an amazingly sexual woman was dancing naked in front of me, I was unable to work up an erection. At this point I was really concerned that, even beyond the SSRI side effects, I was dealing with something deeper.

Turns out it was deep. This is where the *Sexual Intelligence* book came into play.

What started happening in this case was first, absolutely the best sex of my life, and second, my inability to orgasm over the course of five to ten "sessions." WHAT? This had never happened. Talking to my psychiatrist, I was happy to observe,

"Well, I've never had such a sexualized girlfriend at the same time that I ramped up the SSRIs. It makes a huge difference."

I began to learn more about sex than I thought possible. I was pretty sure I was the most sexual/sensual person on the planet. But I had to learn that MY ORGASM was unimportant in the larger scheme of things. What I learned in these few months of confusion was this: SEX is everything that happens before, during, and after orgasm, and orgasm is neither the goal nor required for an amazing sex life. I mean, I love orgasms, but I had to either get over that expectation or get into some funk about sex. And I'll tell you again, I was having the best sex of my life. What? I was confused and a bit frustrated.

A few new tools I learned at this time, besides the deferred focus on my own orgasm, was that men are quite adept at masturbation.

First new learning: Our hand is the most familiar sexual partner we will ever have. Sometimes the friction, speed, and unpredictability of sex with a partner make orgasm difficult. Sounds like heresy. Jacking off might be better than making love. The function of orgasm as a release and the hand as the vehicle is pretty mechanical.

Second new learning: Showing my partner what it looks like when I do masturbate gives her clues about how I like to be touched. I had a bit of resistance to showing her. As we experimented and talked about all that was going on, I read *Why Men Fake It*, by Abraham Morgentaler, and learned our practice with our hands is sort of like our sexual training. So showing her what it looked like when I was doing myself was very good information for her. Good information indeed.

Third new learning: Anorgasmia is a thing. And for a while it was amazing how often I was ready to go again. Without the release of orgasm, I had no refractory period. She loved that.

But eventually she also grew concerned with our sex, if I wasn't coming.

Fourth new learning: As far as sexual experience and my own sexual training is concerned, I was hyper-tuned to her pleasure. Most of my sex life was about extending my time doing her so she could have orgasms. AFTER she was DONE, I'd go for my own. Her-centric sex is fine, but it's a bit shallow. By focusing on her body, her orgasm, and her experience, I was kind of leaving my own enjoyment out for a good portion of our sex. I learned to let myself feel my own body, at this point. Just feel, don't do.

Fifth new learning: The connection is everything. As I had to learn to focus on my pleasure, I also learned that really tuning into the WE of sex, rather than the SHE and ME, was a way of really enjoying things at a deeper level. And we both had some learning to do around pleasing the other person simply for enjoyment rather than our own release.

Summing up good sex

The connection between two people during sex (foreplay, function, and afterplay) is more important than any goal of orgasm.

When orgasm is an issue, sex can still have all the fantastic qualities. In fact, I have been able to have more sex, and have sex longer, which was something I was missing in my normally functioning sex life. (By the way, I'm off the SSRI, and the effortless orgasm has returned for me.)

Knowing what does it for you and being able to show or tell your partner are key ingredients for evolved sex. As we can let go of traditional SEX as the goal and open up to the full range of erotic experiences, we can expand our pleasure and our sexual vocabularies.

What I Learned About Sex: It's Almost All in Your Mind 45

9.

Building the Perfect Lover: 13 Touch Points on the Path to Relationship

If I had the lover I imagine, I'm sure my head would explode in a shower of sparks. I dream, I write, I pray, and I search for the right woman. But mostly I imagine her in crazy-amazing projections and poems and flights of fancy. I know that they are my fantasies, and somehow that keeps me safe. But in building the perfect lover for the next relationship, I do have touch points that are essential for me. I wanted to capture a few of them, for myself, and for gaining a deeper understanding of the core wants and desires of my heart. (Your needs and dreams may vary.)

1. The spark of desire

Something in the way she moves… The spark is an initial reaction to the other person's entire presence. We call it chemistry, lust, passion, sexual desire. But I know what it is when I feel it, and I can tell very quickly when I don't. For all the work ahead to actually build a friendship and relationship, the spark must be genuine. The chemistry does not grow over time, in my experience. Either you know it or you don't. She will have that magical element for me, something I can't name, something that's not about hair, or clothes, or fitness. She will have moves that draw me in even as she's merely crossing the coffee shop to say hello for the first time.

2. A temple of worship

Yes, the physical body is a temple. And for the long haul, I believe that my worship of the feminine body is part of my energy, gift, power, drive. I love women. I have loved very few women. I know that my next full-on love is out there. And I will be patient and honest in my quest to identify and seek her out. But there is not one perfect body. In fact, I'm learning more recently how younger and uber-fit women are no longer turn-ons for me. They remind me of my daughter more than a potential partner. I love watching them run by, all abs and legs and glowing skin. But that's not what I'm looking for. And I think my architectural requirements for that woman are fairly flexible. I know that the combined ingredients outweigh any flash of beauty and brilliance of hip or smile. Still, there is something I want, and all the many ways that I can pay respects to her beauty, the more deeply I will bond. I do have to admit, I am somewhat selective in what I consider beautiful, but it's not the typical hottie. And while this aspect is 100% critical, once I've imprinted on her, she will know I am done, settled, satisfied, as I will tell her all the time and show her in my actions and support.

3. Hopes, dreams, and desires

What does she want? How is she expressing her vibrance in the world? Can she articulate her wants and desires? Does she know what she's looking for in a relationship, and can she express those ideas to me? Clarity of purpose is one of life's true missions. If she is on her own mission, I am much more likely to want to nuzzle up beside her and explore her wants and dreams and how they might or might not dovetail into mine.

4. Holistic intelligence

There is no such thing as just-in-time intelligence. If she is smart, it will show. If she is fascinated by learning and growing, it is easy to see. I listen for some key indicators early in the first coffee date. Is TV a thing for her? If so, we're probably not a match. Doe she have other things to talk about besides work and working out? Can she listen and engage in subjects as we jump quickly from topic to topic? You can even tell when you begin the opening communications via texts or emails. Is there poetry in her words, in how she expresses herself?

5. Brilliant wit

While I love to make a woman laugh, and it may be one of my gifts, I am more interested in how she might make me laugh. Can she engage in rapid-fire banter? If she jokes about something deep, does she get hurt when you joke back? What are the little things that tickle her? Does she laugh easily and often? Laughter might bring me closer to a woman faster than anything else.

6. Eyes that shine like diamonds

Intensity and desire are radiated out of the eyes. You can see excitement, lust, sadness, joy. The women I meet who are alive and radiant are broadcasting on all channels with their eyes. And often makeup can be a distraction, camouflage. On dating profiles, it's the eyes and the smile that draw me in past the initial "curb appeal" profile photo. You can see it even in photos. She's either on fire inside or she's not.

7. Affection

How easily does she show affection? Can she tell you early on what she wants, what she likes, how she likes it? Can she tell you, "Wow, you're cute," or "Man, you are sexy right now." Not in the first few minutes. But if there is an arm brush or a light pat on the shoulder during the first date, then we might have a match with our love language. This woman is going to be my next long-term cheerleader; she needs to be able to share her enthusiasms and ecstasies.

8. Joy that radiates

You can see it, can't you? When someone shines with joy, their beauty is amplified 10-fold. A joyous partner is critical if that's your normal state as well. I've been in two marriages that had an imbalance in the *joi de vivre,* in the simple love of waking up in the morning to see what comes next. I am listening for her joy. I am tuning into the way she expresses herself in all types of situations. We can't always be love and light, but it's easy to notice when someone deals with adversity from a place of security and inner joy.

9. High intensity/low drama

I'm a Type A personality. And while I'm not only attracted to other "driven" people, that might be an unconscious requirement. Certainly drama is the biggest turn off there is. We had enough drama in our previous relationships. We might've stayed in that stressful situation for longer than we should've. But as newly released adults, we should have very low tolerance for drama. It's simply not a necessary tool to communicate wants and needs. In my experience, most drama comes from unmet expectations. And in our busy, two-family lives, expectations are going to be shifted, and disappointments are going to happen. If there's a fiery response to a missed date opportunity due to family obligations, well… perhaps our priorities aren't in sync. Let's put our kids' priorities ahead of our dating priorities, and our expectations can come back to reality. I expect an honest and intense woman who doesn't need to freak out to get her way. I am most likely doing my best to accommodate and appreciate all of the opportunities with her, but things come up. How she responds says a lot about how she will respond in the future.

10. Silent affection

The in-between times. Silences together and silences apart. Are you both okay with a bit of silence? The quiet moments are often the closest. Breathe together and quit trying so hard to figure it out. If she can do that, we're a long way towards compatibility. And her silences just make her that much more mysterious and alluring to me.

11. Love language = Touch

I show my affection by touching you. A pat on the shoulder, a hand on your back, holding hands, are all high forms of affection for me. I have been married twice to women who had other requirements to feel loved. Although the relationship is possible with someone who requires a different language, there is sure to be a lot more negotiation and compromise. I dated a woman once who also spoke "touch." Her open expression of affection for me brought me a new meaning for feeling loved. I could tell she was in love. She let me know, even early on, that she was crazy about me. It felt so different from my last 20 years in adult relationships that I was surprised by how good it made me feel. I have seen what that feels like. A woman with the same love language (touch) is essential for me. Back when I got married, both times, this knowledge hadn't been articulated. Today we have the book (Gary Chapman's *The 5 Love Languages*) and the concept, and we'd better listen to the language of our hearts, because it's going to drive a good portion of our relationship.

12. Spiritual heights

Spiritual and religious are two different things in my mind. One revolves around church, dogma, and some concept of "their god" who is different from the other gods of the world. Christianity is a great example. I was raised Presbyterian. I am a member of a Methodist church. But I rarely go to church. And while I believe Christ was a man, and the Bible does its best to relate his mystical relationship to god and his followers, I don't believe that Christ is the only path to my personal connection to god, or GOD.

I love the people in my church; some are my closest friends. I am deeply moved by the minister nearly every time I hear him speak. But somewhere deep inside of me, I don't need church to feel right with god. My GOD may be different from your GOD, but I believe we're talking about the same deity. Spirituality to me is a form of modern-day mysticism. I believe, like many of the ancient mystics, that our relationship to god, or the beloved, or great spirit, is much more about my personal faith and my relationship to that idea of wholeness. I believe I am communing with my god when I am walking in nature. I believe that a poem is as good as any prayer. So I pray, I write poems, I worship directly through acts of service and appreciations and gratefulness. I often don't go to church.

13. Flexible body and mind

Every item above is an idea of what I want in a relationship. And each one is like a map ready to be set on fire. When SHE shows up, and we begin to explore our connections, the items on my list will magically fade away. While I believe the maps are important to help me identify my priorities, the fulfillment of those ideals will probably come in a form very different from what I imagine. Can this woman be flexible in her ideas and concepts of what she's looking for as well? If she has a construct of no kids, six-pack abs, and radiant smile, we're a non-starter anyway. But in the more subtle ways, can she bring up and let go of dreams, fantasies, hopes, plans? I can, to some degree, and it's this flexibility that keeps me growing and learning even through setbacks, dashed dreams, and disappointments. Those things are going to happen. Conflict is going to happen. But the flexible person can see both sides of an issue and let go of the argument when it no longer serves as a request for change.

Epilogue

I believe in order to find our lover we need a fairly clear picture of that potential person. Way beyond looks, the construction or destruction happens over the course of the initial weeks of "dating." What forms beyond the initial chemistry is what will remain beyond the heat of the sexual newness. If you're addicted to the "next lover," you may pass up the opportunity to explore and educate yourself on ways your maps and strategies are wrong.

To this end, this is more of a prayer than a map. My desires are a bit more abstract, more driven by the heart, less like tactics or requirements. Every map I've created has been torn to shreds by the woman who shows up. That's the idea. But the visualization and wish list are critical structures to understanding your own heart. If you have a map, at least you will know when you've gone off plan, or if you are forging new territories.

10.

Sexual Power, Sexual Prime, Sexual Freedom

Sex can go off the rails in a marriage or any relationship. But it's important to reclaim your sexual energy. And after divorce, that challenge is both difficult and enlightening. Liberated sex between consenting adults is pretty cool. You now have time to figure out what you want, what you need, and what you crave. What better way to understand yourself than in action, in relationship, in sex?

First, let's just talk about sex for a minute. Sex may not be everything, but it is *a lot* of what makes a relationship work. Something about that connection, the oxytocin, the skin time, the gaze into your partner's eyes, gives most of us the boost to return to the world and conquer our fears and enemies.

As sex begins to fall into a routine in your marriage, there are things you can, and should, do to enliven the passion. However, troubles in the relationship often show up early in sex. When you notice, for the first time, that your partner of nine-plus years is waiting for you to finish, it's a bit heartbreaking. Something else was on her mind.

It is true that sex is one of the experiences that strips you of your armor and defensiveness, if you let it. When you begin protecting, or hiding some part of your emotional life, sex is the place you will be found out. Or you will show signs of disinterest, which could be worse. I can't say what it was the first time my then-wife checked out during sex, but I recall the moment exactly.

In the months that followed, I began noticing her entire attitude towards sex was changing. Not only was she less likely to take me up on my offers for affection, she was irritated (and this was entirely new) with some of my attempts to please her. She complained once with such anger that I was discouraged and hurt. Where normally she might guide me to a better angle, or type of rub, she was just mad. I tried to leap over the hurt with enthusiasm, but I now see that she was exhibiting her frustration at something a lot bigger than my technique.

So… as it happens, sex went south on us, and eventually we got divorced. Of course, we didn't get divorced because of the downhill momentum of our sexual relationship, but the sex, or lack of sex, was a pretty clear indicator of how we were losing touch with each other.

Divorced. All is new again. We get a chance, or chances, to do it all over again. We have an opportunity to be with new women, where we once imagined our horizon only contained one. It's not all that easy to get back into the swing of things, a lot has changed, but when we do, when we begin to feel sexual again, all kinds of good things happen.

Once I began having sex again, I was amazed at how much energy I got from it. Sure, there was the post-sex drowsies, but my ego and self-esteem began to show signs of life again. I remember walking around a new woman's house, completely naked and proud. Happy we were connected and connecting. Sure, this one was not for the "relationship" books, but it was an awakening nonetheless. Sex began to remind my brain of all the good things that come from being in "relationship."

Lot's of good chemicals are released during sex and even during simple touching and cuddling. If you are a touch-based person (see *Love Languages*), your well-being and joy come from skin-to-skin contact, or SKIN TIME. It's important.

And even as the act of sex has changed, and often orgasm is neither the goal nor the endpoint, the benefits of a newly rejuvenated sex drive cannot be underestimated. So can we get addicted to sex? Can the euphoric chemicals associated with orgasm become a necessary craving that disables us when it is taken away? Maybe. I don't know the science around it, but losing my skin time with my wife was the saddest part of the drifting apart for me.

Nowadays, the online dating sites give hope for more relationship opportunities on the horizon. The navigation of them can lead to a lot of misses, but if you understand yourself and what you are looking for, the effort can be worth the hassle.

Then, wouldn't being single be a preference? Wouldn't having opportunities to be with more different partners be better than trying to find THE ONE again? Are we reaching our new sexual prime as we are liberated from painful marriages and back into the dating pool of partners who may also crave skin time?

Knowing yourself better, you can begin to form some ideas of what you are looking for. Are you looking for the NEXT relationship? Are you looking to date or find several women who are interested in FWB or NSA-sex? (Vocabulary: FWB = friends with benefits, and NSA = no strings attached.)

I would have to say, my inclination is to go for the ONE. Not necessarily the NEXT ONE, the ONLY ONE, or the NEXT WIFE, but I've had a hard time in the past keeping my dating life sorted out if it involved more than one woman at a time. But I'm being challenged on that concept. Why? There ARE other women. There are plenty of women and plenty of time. And when my kids fly the nest, in six or seven years, I'll have even more time. So what's my need to jump back into an exclusive relationship again?

I don't know. A lot of things are lined up against that idea, or at least in favor of multiple experiences, multiple partners, and multiple boosts in the old chemical cornucopia of good and joyful sex. I mean, think about it. We're kind of back to safe sex as older folks; we may not have to worry about birth control. We have some ideas of what we like and what we don't like. And perhaps a new partner would introduce us to some ideas we hadn't ever thought of.

So why the serial monogamy? What's so great about marriage that we would do it again, either actually or in practice? Are we giving away some of our power, some of our access to the tonic resources of sexual connection by limiting ourselves in our old-world thinking? Or is sex with someone you love, real-connected-sex, something different and desirable?

Today it's hard for me to know the answer. But I do know that the power of sex is back, and I don't want to give it up now any more than I did when my marriage began to falter. This time, I don't have to suffer when things go off the rails. I can just pack up and move along to another potential mate. Is this bad? Is this more animal? Or is this the modern version of dating after divorce?

11.

Our Sexual Brain and the Lies it Tells Us

At the base of the relationships between men and women is the animal nature. The physiology and biology that propelled us out of the caves and into the stars are still really about hormones, chemicals in the brain, and our unquenchable desire to further our genetic lines. Even as evolved as we think we are, chemicals like testosterone and dopamine really affect more of our energy and motivation than we'd like to think.

I've been exploring my own fixation on youth and fitness and how that is largely driven by these same procreative, base needs. And how as a somewhat evolved male homo sapiens, I have some control over the more ape-like ancestral rushes that occasionally course through me. Today I hit on an example that might clarify a bit more of my self-examination around these urges versus what I really want.

Today I was playing tennis with my 11-year-old daughter. I have been teaching her how to play. Today on the court I was sitting back and watching her practice serves. On the court next to us was an older woman who, though sightly more robust than my partnering preference, was doing a fine job of beating the pants off her male partner. Just outside the fence behind my daughter, a young coed, walking her dog, strolled by looking quite fit, but perhaps a bit young to be of interest other than an observation of her beauty.

Seeing these three women at the same time, I got it in a flash.

My animal brain and body were attracted to the coed. My love and parenting body was happily enjoying my daughter's physical practice. And my mind, unencumbered by sexual fantasy, was also fascinated and interested in the woman playing tennis.

The sirens of sex.

I don't have to give in to the sexual chemistry. And one thing I know about myself, when I'm getting some of my sexual needs met, my sublimated sexual energy is much less powerful. I've been trying to understand some of this dynamic in myself as I'm trying to imagine and conjure up my next relationship.

Before I was paired up, as a boyfriend or a married man, I was a bit more like a wild animal. Every flash of cleavage, every picture on the web, all the titillation around me would give stir to my ape-chemistry, and I would derive a little motivational boost. It wasn't that I wanted to mate with each of the objects of desire, but there was some shortage in my life, some lack. Perhaps my ape-brain was looking for a mate. My evolved-brain was a bit more capable of parsing out the desire part from the sex part, and I was usually able to leave the potential mate unmolested.

But something cool happened when I got mated up. (And I am certain this is different for each man and woman, as we all have different histories and hoped-for futures.) When I was IN relationship, I no longer scanned the savannah for sex. I could see an attractive young athlete and say, "Wow," but I no longer had any desire to pursue sex or children or even gawking at her.

That's how I knew, in my evolved self, that Girlfriend 1 was not the IT girl for me. Even as I was in relationship with her, and committed to her, my ape-related drive was not satisfied. Even though I had a relationship with an attractive woman, my chemistry was not settled. I did not feel completed.

I know that's a bad metaphor. But something in my DNA likes to be mated. And when it is complete, or solid, I no longer cruise the herd looking for something fresh, new, and young. When I was married, even as things were going south, there was never a moment when I considered pursuing sex with another woman. I simply did not want anything, sexually, other than what I had. So, like an animal, when the sex went south, too, I began to express my rage and sadness and loss.

It's interesting to note, as creatures of chemistry and instinct, we are also driven by motivation, safety, and happiness. I am certain that part of my happiness was related to the sex and the chemicals it produced, the safety and trust it expressed, so that when lost, I began to wonder for the first time about the viability of my relationship.

I never looked outside the marriage for that connection. And even after divorced I maintained a fairly celibate life, as I knew my sexual-brain could get me into a lot of trouble when it was flooded with so much sadness, anger, and appetite.

I had never been adored like I was adored by Girlfriend 1. She was fearless, close, and spoke "touch" as her love language as well. I tried to get a clue about my sexual ennui over the three months of our relationship, and in the end agreed to release her back to the wild so she could find the roar for her that was as strong as her roar for me.

Today I connected a tiny bit more of my history and chemistry. And I identified the Sexual Sirens that are all around me and saw for the first time how different they were to me, depending on my relationship status. If I was mated and getting regular sex, I could ignore their siren song. If I was alone, like a lone lion, I was eager to catch thrill and quick to give chase.

I knew when I was married that I was SET. I did not desire another woman, ever. I did not roam or roar for anyone else. But when the sexual connection was severed, I roared like a wounded animal and fell into a long period of rebuilding.

Along those lines, then, my thinking is, when I'm sorting out and evaluating my next relationship, I will listen to the clues in my body and my brain that are either satisfied or hungry to guide a part of my understanding of the animal fit. There's a lot more to a RELATIONSHIP than fit or chemistry, but boy, when those things go off, there's a lot of roaring to do.

12.

Three Loves: Eros, Filial, Agape

I've been trying to create a lover from thin air. Using all my conjuring powers, all my musical and romantic tricks to summon the next great lover. And... I'm not sure I have been doing it right. I learned something this morning as I revved forward into a peaceful Sunday morning, alone.

At church I was listening and not listening to the sermon. I had not been in over a year. I did love this preacher and this feeling of home that was comfort and solace in my past joys and pains. But for brief moments I was trolling. I was scanning the entire church for attractive women. WHAT?

Sid was giving a sermon on love. WHAT? Maybe it was time to give my search a rest and listen. Maybe this morning was no random occurrence. And in my somewhat mixed state, I listened and scanned. But I became aware of the frivolousness of my longing. The Type A searching, which had produced ZERO ecstatic partners, might not be serving me. What if I relaxed. Sat back. And grooved on being present and lovable. Loveable even to myself.

The words from a song by the band Bush kept running through my head: "**Breathe in, breathe out, breathe in, breath out...**"

So, there was one woman. She was familiar. She had been part of the church for at least five years. She had joined as a recently divorced mom with a three-year-old daughter. She was beautiful.

Eros

Eros is often thought of as the love of sex. But it's much more than sexual. It's the fire, the passion, the drive to create. Noticing that much of my eros or erotic energy was focused on finding a partner, I could understand how that energy was being funneled away from the other creative passions. My attempts to create the lover I wanted, to woo in a certain way that the other person became inflamed at the same level, were draining some of my resources and some of my beauty with all the effort.

In fact, I wanted to let go and present myself a bit more low key and wait for some of the flame to come from the other person. I wanted patience. Even in the heat and rush of passion, I did not want to be the 90% generator of the flames. I would not create my lover. My lover needed to come fully created and meet me on the field. Anything else was beginning to feel like pushing the river.

Filial love

Filial love is family, community, connectedness. This was the love I was being washed in, sitting alone with friends. Sometimes, in the darkness, even this filial love is not enough, and we'd rather stay in our quiet, dark, boxes and suffer alone. But just knowing that our family was out there, that our filial ties were strong even when we were all silent… Today I felt the family I had been missing. And the love from the family of origin that I had never gotten as a child.

Agape love

This is the flat-out powerful love of the creator, however you care to imagine her. God, Jesus, Mohammed... Native American gods. All part of the whole. The GOD of gods. However you chose to believe, however you chose to be amazed, that is the god of Agape. And while it can be sustaining, it is not nourishing in the same way as the first two. And certainly not as filling and energetic as the first one, Eros.

So if I am running around, poetry-ing, wooing, sending love letters to someone I hope to awaken, perhaps I am draining some of the essence that I could be using elsewhere, if I just relaxed into the process. Time is the key. Time is everything. And timing is important too.

Let's look at the woman in the congregation. She was obviously attractive to me and known to me. She was the only sexually attractive person in the congregation of about 120 people. And that's it. We caught each other's eye several times. I flirted in my mind and tried to return to the message Sid was delivering. I had mixed results. But I did learn something.

> 1. I found 1 person out of 120 people sexually attractive.
>
> 2. Her physical beauty was what drew my attention in, as I was scanning.
>
> 3. What I knew about her, other than her initial introduction to the church, was nothing. She was alone today, but that's all I could tell.
>
> 4. She smiled at me. Or was she smiling in my direction? Hard to know.

If I had been determined and focused on finding a partner, I might have stayed after church and initiated a conversation with her. I didn't.

This one attractive person was amazing, and the revelation of my above-average tastes was also revealing.

It was not her. I was too intent on looking for someone. Perhaps I was too intent on "creating" someone who loved me back. But my impatience could lead me to a lot of unnecessary churn.

I learned something from what Sid said about marriage today and the line of the marriage vow, the part about "until death do us part." It seems so archaic today. Do we really believe in marriage, or that vow, with today's marriage statistics?

What I learned, or heard at least, was that this vow was more about commitment. Could we commit to wanting and working towards a love that would last? That we could put ourselves all in, and vow to do whatever it takes to keep the relationship and love growing, in spite of setbacks personal, financial, and physical? Could we say YES to the full thrust of the LOVE we were being asked to participate in?

It's food for thought. I don't know about marriage. I don't know what the ring and the vows mean today, in my life. But I do understand the commitment, beyond all measure, to continue the search for love and loving within the entire arc of our relationship. Where it will all lead, that is more of a mystery. But when she shows up before me and says, "YES," I won't hesitate. I will know. But I can't go out questing for her. I can't write poems to capture her. I cannot make her into the lover I imagine.

Trying is not fair to either of us.

13.

It's Always About Time

Last night I began to get the picture.

I spent a casual evening with one of the women with potential. And the contrast could not have been more pronounced. There was no kissing, no driven agenda, but just spending time together.

When the desire is there, and the feelings necessary to connect, the next ingredient is time.

If both participants don't put forth the effort to make time for the relationship to grow… That's the answer right there.

Just this week, the smiling girl backed out of an opportunity. I offered additional options and texted her the next day. There were no plans to be made. I'm fine with being the initiator, but I won't be the only one putting out the offers. It's very telling when the other person stops offering ideas.

So she's gone quiet.

And often I would be the one, like a puppy dog, doing somersaults to try and interest someone in the "next thing." But not today. If the mutual effort is not there, that may be the biggest tell of all. Once the effort is not mutually beneficial, the energy for making it happen gets lopsided. And it DOES feel like a game. A bit. This idea of not calling because you put the last offer in and got no response. But it's also a very subtle system of energy and intention.

1. Smiling girl is quite a runner. She makes time, every day, for running. She is distressed if she misses a day in her routine.

2. Our first meeting was facilitated because she was too tired to run, so why don't we get together.

3. We had some fun at our first date and second date, where we had lunch on Mother's Day.

4. She backed out of our next opportunity, because she was late getting back into town and was feeling tired…

5. The next night, I texted her around the end of the day, "Just saying hi, seeing what's next…"

6. We exchanged pleasantries. She loves to compliment my humor. "Ha ha ha ha."

7. Nothing.

In my equation, she interrupted the flow. It's okay, I was stretching to see if I could actually be with a beautiful but non-creative person. (The jury is still out on that concept.) But I felt a bit of a loss. I was looking forward to accepting that kissing offer she put out after our first "date."

I am also aware that I was ready to engage in less-than-100%. For some reason (loneliness, thrill, change of pace), I was willing to move things forward, even when I had my doubts about the real value of the relationship potential. I think I was infatuated with her neck.

Contrast this with the wonderful developments of the second woman with potential, who's presented herself again as interested.

1. We had made casual plans to go out on Saturday night.

2. Mid-afternoon Friday, she said, "I had something else come up on Sat. Sorry. But I'm available tonight."

3. She would contact me after a professional networking party she needed to attend.

4. When she did contact me, we checked in. She had stated earlier that she was not too full of energy at the moment. We made plans, even at 9:30.

5. I came to her house without pomp or circumstance. She had gotten a DVD of a movie she wanted to see. We sat on the couch. We held hands. We chatted, laughed, and enjoyed each other's company.

6. She walked me to my car at midnight, when I was heading home. We held hands as we walked.

7. I mentioned my joy at the evening, "Massively casual."

8. "Yes."

There was no need in my book to try and confirm or set up a future time together. The time with her was easy, close, and yes… casual.

I've said to her in several calls and emails that while I'm intentional, I am not ambitious or driven to move things along with her. I'm more interested in being with her. Spending time with someone I like. I'm fascinated by her. That is enough.

She is responsive. She is private and protective of her space and time. And she has some magical combination of massive sensuality and creative writerly fantasy woman. DANGER! (I kid myself!)

It's easy for me to imagine how I could fall in love with her. But the first step is just time. Time before the adoration sets in. Time doing simple and mundane things. Mutually arranged and beneficial time together. It's easy to feel confident when the effort to find another time flows from both sides. If it's only one partner, the balance shifts in some fundamental way.

It's important to me that the reaching out is mutual. Last night while we were side by side on the couch, she also reached out and held or stroked my arm from time to time. It was non-sexual, it was awesome, it was just pure affection. I cannot generate that myself. I can draw it in, ask for it, and attempt to stir it up in her, but the reaching out (or reaching back) is up to the other person.

The other woman with potential said something in one of our overthinking sessions, "Because if it did develop into a relationship, there's then going to be more demand for time. More desire for time together."

Yes.

14.

Seven Signs of a Healthy Post-Divorce Relationship

Divorce is hard. Dating after divorce is tricky too, and I've found some things I think are good indicators of how whole a person is and how ready that person is for a healthy relationship. Sure, your dating profile says something like, "Let's be friends first and see where that takes us." But most people I meet are really hoping that friendship takes us to the next wave of affection. I think we are mostly looking to be found and appreciated by another person, while having the opportunity to appreciate that person back. We want to become the most fantastic cheerleader for their hopes and dreams, and we expect that positive affirmation in return.

We don't need a relationship. We want one. We are fine alone. We have found our own way out of the desert of depression and despair. And now, standing strong and alone again, we are ready to dip our toes into the idea of being loved and loving again. It is a huge risk. And some people can't get over it. Their divorce is still too painful, or their relationship with their ex is still too volatile. They are really not ready for a relationship.

If, however, you begin to think your shit is sufficiently together to date again, some new boundaries are in order. And here are what I've found to be the indicators of a healthy start.

1. The relationship with the ex is business-like and

drama-free.

If your potential partner is still dramatically engaged or enraged at the ex-partner, watch out. You are likely to take some of the "stand-in" damage for the anger that needs a place to dissipate. Irritation and conflict can always arise. But pay attention to how this person deals with these setbacks or conflicts. It's likely this is how any future conflict with you might evolve, as well. Are they able to articulate what the problem is? Can they negotiate a solution and then let it go? The emotional baggage from divorce is huge. And it's tough to get through all the processing that needs to happen before we can cut it loose and be free of the burden of our ex.

2. The other person puts the kids ahead of the relationship.

In my experience, I find a potential partner who has had kids (they can be older or younger than mine) is more likely to be accepting and accommodating of my relationship with my kids. When my kids call, they come first. Sure, it's an interruption, and it puts the "special friend" in a secondary role, but it's clear to me that my kids' emotional and physical well-being is much more important than my having a girlfriend. Especially at this point in my life, while they are still in school and still very much under my influence. I have a deep respect for my role model as a dad and as a man. I am showing both my daughter and my son how a man acts in the world. Even under duress, I am showing how I can remain calm and make strong and positive decisions. And always, my kids come first. Especially in the early stages of a new relationship.

3. In meeting the kids, there are no major hangups or obvious attachment issues.

Divorce traumatizes all of the family members. And often this trauma causes us to revert to old and unhealthy defense mechanisms. And of course, as a divorced and now-single parent, I am going to do everything I can to take care of my kids' needs. BUT... this has to be carefully done. I have seen both men and women who were WAY too enmeshed with their children. Maybe the kid was a brat who was completely undisciplined. Or perhaps the child was overly shy and withdrawn, folding himself or herself into the parent. At younger ages some of this behavior is acceptable. But as the child ages and reaches the end of elementary school, the child should not need to be coddled or babied because the other parent is trying to make up for some loss. The single parent cannot make up for the divorce. But everyone survives and moves on. Both the kids and the parents need to return to healthy boundaries and healthy communication styles, so that everyone can grow up and let go of the stigma and shame of the divorce.

4. Conversations about divorce, parenting, or relationships are not tense.

In early stages of a relationship, most of the time you want to hear, "What happened?" And this opportunity to share your story and hear the divorce story of the other person is a great time to listen for their response. How have they accepted their own responsibility for the divorce? Even if the divorce was the result of some infidelity, have they been able to move beyond the anger? The best approach to the ex is to live and let be. Focus on the kids. Walking away from a marriage is hard work, and the way someone tells their divorce story is important. Listen.

5. Clarity of intention and honest expression of affection and desire

You'd think that if someone is dating again, that person is ready for a relationship. But that's often not the case. You'd even imagine that someone who puts up a dating profile online, and who talks about what they want in their next relationship, probably has some intention of being in a relationship. You might be wrong. I have been on quite a few dates where the women had no idea what they wanted. I had one woman, whom I connected with and had just spent nearly two hours talking to, tell me in the parking lot as she was getting into her car, "I can tell you at least three reasons I'm not right for you." She didn't, but she said she knew she had no real idea of what she wanted in a relationship. If you're dating, be clear on if you want to "date" or have a relationship. I've heard that some people are into casual dating and casual sex. That's never worked for me, but if that's your thing, make sure that's what the other person is saying as well. People who cannot give you a good idea of what they are looking for, how their next relationship might look or feel, may not be ready to be in a relationship. And if you can't articulate what you are looking for, if you are vague, or simply lonely, you might want to keep working on yourself and your approach to relationships before jumping right back into one.

6. Alcohol and TV are not constant sources of entertainment or escape.

Drinking together can be fun, but it shouldn't be a lifestyle choice, unless you are both into it. If the person doesn't really open up until a glass of wine or two, you might be rubbing up against someone who has a hard time expressing herself. In moderation, as a celebration lifter, a few drinks on the weekend are no problem. But if it's every single night, and the glass of whatever becomes like the cup of coffee in the morning, a necessary lubricant, there is probably an issue there. And I've seen TV become the same sort of numbing or escaping addiction. I went on a few dates with a woman who professed an addiction to reality TV shows. She also turned around and fought with me about the virtues of TV overall, and how TV was no less interactive than reading a book or playing a game with someone. Um.... yeah. Escapism should not be a common theme. You want clear and present as the normal relating condition between you and another consenting adult.

7. Affection that moves into sexual relations doesn't change the overall tone of the friendship.

Of course you'd like to be friends first. And if the chemistry is working, there may be a pull towards the bedroom. But you need to know that if you are looking for a relationship, sex, while important, is not the most important aspect of a relationship. You are going to be spending a lot of time with this person out of the bedroom doing other things, and you'd be better off seeing if your "out of the sack" experience is good too. Don't get me wrong, a good sexual chemistry is a powerful motivator. But don't let the sex cloud your understanding of who the person is and what other things you like to do together. You can't screw all the time.

And initiation of sex shouldn't cause major shifts in the relationship. Your friendship should still remain a focus in all of the stages of a relationship. Perhaps that's part of what leads us to divorce; we stop dating our partners and begin to take them for granted. We stop cheerleading and become more of a negotiator, or even antagonist.

Listen to yourself as you talk about the relationship as well. When you are describing your relationship to a friend, notice the words you use. How do you describe this new interest? What are the highlights that you are proud to share about this person?

And listen as you talk to this person as well. Are you open and free with your expressions of affection or desire? Can you say what you need? Are you holding back or withholding some information for fear of upsetting the other person? All of these are clues that the relating part of the relationship still might need some exploration.

Relationships are fun. And now that we have our kids, and our independence, we can be more intentional and clear about what we want in our next relationship. It doesn't have to be about marriage but can be more about learning to love and feel loved again. Take your time. Be intentional with your time, attention, and actions. And if things don't feel right, move along. If you're not in a hurry, there are plenty of fish in the sea and plenty of time to find one that's just right. Or at least better than what you've done before.

III

Children Come First

Sometimes you might feel like you always will be playing second fiddle to his children. But if a dad wants a relationship, he's got to learn to expand his protective armor and let you in. It's not about "us" versus "them." It's about creating a new "we." Children are important, but children grow up and move on. A divorced dad is looking to recreate the marriage he longed for when he had his kids in the first place.

15.

In Relationship With a Divorced Dad: Ground Rules

A woman responded to one of my Single Dad Wants blog posts with a very moving and impassioned comment. I responded,

> Lucky, I really like your comment. Your man, your divorced dad, is lucky to have someone so understanding. And while I only have limited experience with being on the dad's side of the experience, I do have a little knowledge of what you speak.

Plenty of single parents use their kids to get out of almost every obligation. Even obligations to themselves: exercise, dating, taking responsibility for their own actions. And I have been the dad who apologized for checking his phone when a text dinged while on a date. I don't think I will always do this, and at certain moments the phone definitely needs to be turned off, but until my kids are off to college, I'm at least going to make sure there is no emergency. That's the deal with me.

But then there is my response and my boundaries with both my kids and my ex that must be understood and enforced as well. I am available 24/7 for emergencies. But when the text dings and it is, in fact, one of my kids… Well, at this point I have several options. Let's take this from the perspective of a FIRST DATE, rather than a developing relationship. In a first date you are trying to make an impression. That "best behavior" should be the formula for the relationship going forward. Certainly things change as dating evolves into a relationship, but let's take the first date as our benchmark for good behavior, especially on the single dad's side of the dinner table.

Scenario 1: Crisis

If I determine that the issue is a crisis that requires a response, I will apologize, explain the situation briefly, and respond with a text or phone call. From that point on, you should treat it like an unexpected emergency. Everyone's agenda and desires take a backseat to the first aid and trauma response. ("Your daughter has fallen on the playground and needs to see a doctor.") And beware that many requests can be set up like a crisis ("Dad, I need my science binder by 3rd period tomorrow, I left it at your house"), when they are actually poorly formed requests. Your willingness to let these types of requests become new plans can tell a lot about healthy boundaries and good parenting skills.

Scenario 2: Request

The text could be a request from one of the kids or the ex. "Dad can I go home with Kate after school today?" Depending on the situation, you can choose to ignore (the discussion that evening, "You needed to ask me the night before, we've already got plans") or respond. But it's not a crisis. And if you ignore it, no one will be hurt. Frustrated perhaps, but not hurt.

Scenario 3: The ex drops the ball

"Dad, I need someone to pick me up after the cross-country meet and I can't get Mom to pick up." Things happen. We make mistakes. And between strained divorced parents, there can be some manipulation and control going on. Let's assume the best. In this scenario, the kid needs a ride. Whatever the situation, the mom is incommunicado, a problem that might need to be addressed at a different time, and a solution needs to be provided. "Okay, count on me to be there if we can't get your Mom to respond. I'll keep trying her, and you do the same. But OF COURSE, go to your cross-country race, we will figure it out."

Scenario 4: I'd really rather...

Kids can be an excuse to get out of anything. Sorry, but it's true. If your divorced dad is always breaking plans because his kid is sick, getting an award, has a recital… Well, you might want to see why you're no longer a priority. Don't let his kids become an excuse. Make sure the two of you have a chance to establish enough rapport that you can ask, "Dude, if you don't want to go to this event with me, just say it." Kids can be the easy way out. I've done it. I'll probably do it again. Sorry. It's often easier than a confrontation. But if you're avoiding the confrontation because "his kids need him all the time," that might be the issue right there.

Scenario 5: Kids as an excuse

Very similar to Scenario 4. When used in a relationship, the "excuse" is often used to recover from a miss of some sort. "I'm sorry I didn't call you last night. The kids got home and all hell broke loose." That might be okay, if your call was just a "nighty night" check-in, but if you were scheduled to talk about living arrangements, that might be an example of using the kids as an excuse for not taking responsibility.

Scenario 6: Playful kids will be kids only so long.

Kids are our singular priority as parents. As I move into a relationship with another woman, I know that, too, will become a priority. I push back on my kids all the time. They ask, they demand, they whine, they want all kinds of things. That's what kids do. And I know that if I have an opportunity to PLAY with my kids, at this point in my life, I'm going to choose that, whenever possible. But in a primary relationship I also want to PLAY with my partner. The balance between these two desires of mine is more about respect and courtesy than it is about being divorced or not.

As a single dad, I entered in a new dating relationship with a woman who does not have kids. I could feel the pull. We soon had moments of "Oh shit, your kids are there, I'm sorry…" and "Don't worry about the kids, they are in their rooms studying." If I try to imagine her point of view I'd be projecting, so I'll stick with mine.

As a single dad, I do understand that my kids are a priority. That's a given. But kids can be used as an unhealthy defense mechanism as well.

And as I have stated that I didn't think I'd be interested in dating a woman who was not a mom, I've had to revise that statement, based on new information. My fear about dating a woman without kids is more about boundaries and time management. It's not about her being a mother or not. It's not about her wanting more of my attention or not. The issue is about MY management of MY relationship to my kids and my ex-wife and HER.

I can use the kids to get away with murder. With a single mom as a date, I know that she will understand when the kids trump our plans. However, with a date who is not a single mom, the same rule applies. Kids MIGHT trump our plans, but I am always willing to talk about it. And I am perfectly capable of making decisions based on a request and a crisis in the moment.

My goal then, is to keep all requests out of crisis mode. And keep all boundary discussions about us and not the kids. The real answer is: As a single parent I have responsibilities to my kids that will trump all plans 100% of the time. However, I will never use those same responsibilities to disrespect you or avoid my commitment and responsibilities to you. An emergency will be evaluated on a case-by-case basis, and I will always attempt to let you know the real story.

I will try to say, "I'm sorry, sweetheart, I'm just tired and I don't want to go," rather than, "Oh, they moved the parent-teacher conference without telling me, I need to bail on the opera." I'll simply say, "Sorry darling, I don't like opera." We can take the negotiations from there.

Never use your kids as an excuse. But also don't make your kids the reason not to explore a new life, a new relationship, and the new intimacies that may open up a whole new future for you and them, eventually.

16.

Focus on Your Kid's Strengths

Divorce is hard on everyone, especially the kids. And through the process you'll do everything you can to put the positive spin on things to keep them from feeling the full burn of the bad feelings between you and their "other" parent.

This morning when my son texted me that the lead guitar solo in a song (Muse, "Knights of Cydonia") was inspiring him to think about picking up the guitar, I encouraged him. We've been talking about guitar lessons all summer, but he was busy having a summer and taking some online summer school classes. To have him express the desire, out of the blue, was quite a thrill for me. It woke me with a big smile. (He goes to bed at midnight on weeknights, and I'm ALWAYS asleep, since I arise at 6:00 a.m.)

Also this morning, my ex-wife sent me an email detailing the current situation with the kids' teeth. The dentist has got them doing Invisalign and both of them are complaining about pain. WHAT? When did we decide to do braces (even cool high-tech braces) for the kids? She's taken to making decisions without consulting me. This is not in the spirit of co-parenting. And it defies our agreements about the kids and their management and healthcare.

So I said to her, "Neither kid needs braces. Period!"

So while I'm sure that her motivation is more about them than her or me, I'm pretty sure she made the decision 100% without talking to me about it. GRRR.

And still... I was writing about staying focused on your kids so they can develop their own super powers. I'll let them take charge of the situation, with my support. After I sent her the email, I sent my son and daughter this text.

> Today, 9:54 AM
>
> Were the Invisalign braces your idea? Do you still want them?

In our parenting plan we're supposed to agree on these types of actions or they don't happen. So...

Let's see how this develops. The kids are doing fine with their beautiful teeth just as they are. And you should see their smiles. YES, we're doing something right. Co-parenting, maybe, not so much.

17.

The Transcendent Single Father

Relationships come and go. Breakups and divorces happen. Heck, I've had two divorces. The real transformation comes when you have children with a partner. Almost by magic, the shift happens. You're still in love with your partner, but suddenly this other tiny human is sucking up all of your love cycles. You love them both, but push comes to shove, you're going to go with the kid. It's human nature. Nurture, I suppose, is the word. You're going to protect, cuddle, shelter, and encourage this tiny human for the rest of your life.

If the marriage comes to an end, often it is tragic but survivable. The children were the shining point of truth for me. Was I going to give in to the depression and financial crash of the divorce, or was I going to get back up and be the dad I needed to be? My choice was clear. My path to recovery and resurgence was less assured.

At the very beginning of the end I had a tough choice to make. Things had been strained and getting worse between my then-wife and I for almost a year. When she snapped and blurted out in couple's therapy that she had, in fact, gone to see an attorney, I was caught with my proverbial pants down. I knew things were tough. I knew we were more friends and parents than lovers, but DIVORCE? What?

In that very session, she asked me to leave the house. "Give me and the kids some relief. Some quiet time. A little cooling off." Our therapist seemed to agree. Again, another shock. Wait… What?

Time slowed down. My mind flashed back on my parents' divorce and the bloodshed that followed. I had never contemplated divorce from this woman staring angrily, tearfully, at me from across the therapist's office. The both awaited my response.

"No way."

It was early April. Our two children (third and fifth graders) had two months left to go in the school year. And these two people were suggesting we tell them, "Daddy had to go on a business trip." I paused and took a deep breath.

We were not really in couple's therapy. We *were* in therapy, for sure, but it was a slightly different approach. Systems-centered therapy (SCT) is about separating what's real from what are merely feelings and emotions. And while I still respect the therapist deeply for all he was trying to do, he missed the mark on this one. By a long shot.

"Our kids are two months from finishing the school year. We've lived as roommates for six months. I'm sure we can be big enough to share the house until summer break."

They both looked at me with concern and disapproval. We ran out the clock on the session with us agreeing to disagree about this MAJOR POINT in our marriage and eventual divorce. Mind you, this was the first time I learned that my then-wife had been looking at her "options" with a lawyer.

It was the counselor at the kids' elementary school who talked some sense into my then-wife about letting the kids finish the year. "They will need the time to regroup. Don't do it while they still have to come to class every day. Give them some time off in the summer. I've seen this kind of thing really hurt children in the long run."

Yes. We, as the adults in the room, can take the high road and figure our shit out. Our kids needed to finish the year and maybe even have a few weeks of summer before we split the atom.

It was a rough few months. I fluctuated from anger to compassion. I wanted to patch things up, but there was no talk of reconciliation. She was still convinced that maybe a separation would give her some perspective. She dangled it out there like some hope. It was a false hope. She was making plans, doing spreadsheets, and outlining her roadmap towards divorce.

Occasionally we'd cross paths in the hallway and I'd extend my arms, almost by instinct, to hug her before I realized what I was doing. I usually mumbled an apology, "Sorry. I'll figure this out. I'll do better."

As the weeks drew on, it was increasingly difficult to make nice. We could easily disguise our frostiness while getting the kids ready for school, because I was usually the one up and making breakfast and corralling everyone, while my then-wife did her hair and makeup. This was my time, my mastery: joyfully waking, feeding, and delivering my kids to school. The fact that it was our last year as an intact family was known only to myself and my soon-to-be ex-wife.

All this time, over those two months, we were meeting with our "parenting plan" therapist and our "financial split" accountant. And she was meeting with her attorney. Since we had agreed not to fight over anything, I didn't seek legal advice at that time.

We examined our combined estate from three scenarios:

1. She keeps the house and pays me for the equity,

2. I keep the house and pay her for the equity, or

3. We sell the house and split the equity.

In the divorce therapist's office, we began to talk about what was "in the best interest of the children."

In this collaborative process of divorce I was a bit naive. I trusted that we were negotiating with everyone's interest at heart. I was misled. As it turns out, my then-wife knew, and the divorce therapist knew, but I did not know, that we were going straight for the divorce-in-Texas package. See, traditionally men have been assholes as well as the primary breadwinner. And traditionally, the mom has been the shelter and love provider and perhaps even the stay-at-home family hub. For us, the stay-at-home-mom plan was sort of how we initially set out on our parenting journey together. However, I was no absent father. That had been how my dad was.

The part missing, the heart of my relationship and my agreement with my then-wife, was that we would parent these children 50/50 with all of our love and focus. Everything in our lives revolved around being the best parents we could be. I handled the first half of the day (wake up, breakfast, and school), and she handled the afternoon. We both wanted the kids to have a parent home when they got off the school bus. And we were 100% successful in that accomplishment. I believe our kids still show the resilience of that decision. We parented 50/50 because that's how we believed our kids would become balanced individuals themselves.

In the divorce therapist's office, however, the story changed. Questions about our parenting responsibilities became much more loaded. And I was challenged on my ability to fix dinner. What? Seriously? I tried to push back, "And what about mornings and breakfast and getting the kids to school? How much of that responsibility have you had in the morning, over the last five years?" I was a very conscious and present dad. I was not the absent father, and she was not the stay-at-home mom. We *had* been doing parenting 50/50, just as we planed.

Divorce however, is not about what's fair, or what's real. Divorce is a battle. Even in the most positive divorce, with the most friendly parents, things can get messy pretty quickly when you're talking about the rest of your lives with your children. I'm guessing her maternal instinct kicked in.

The conversation about the schedule and parenting plan changed dramatically. When things got too heated, the therapist would talk to each of us individually to reset. In one of these cooling periods, she leveled with me, "Here's what she's going to get if you guys go to court."

And it was at this very second, when my heart was shattered and broken, that I gave up. I didn't mean to. I didn't know what else to do. The toll of the two months of guarded living had broken my fighting spirit.

Maybe I had done enough. Maybe some of the wisdom about the "mom" and the nurturing was true in our case, even if it didn't feel as lopsided as the term *non-custodial parent* indicated. I was facing my divorce therapist alone. And she was looking at me and saying things like "in the best interest of the kids" and "most fathers react this way."

I was NOT most fathers.

We tore up the 50/50 schedule that I brought into the counseling session. We started again with the SPO (standard possession order) and the non-custodial rights and responsibilities. And although I gave up a huge piece of my "dad time" that day, I've never stopped working to show up for my kids at every opportunity afforded me. That I am afforded that opportunity only 31% of the time, instead of 50%, is an issue. But that was not the time to fight. Or if it was, I was not capable of another battle. And the therapist was looking at me, sharing her compassion with me, and telling me, "This is what she's going to get. Let's start here."

Today I'm certain I would try to do it differently, given the chance. And perhaps in the near future I will be given an opportunity to reset the schedule. But the damage was done, and the divorce proceeded with all the typical restrictions and legalese. When I did consult a divorce attorney, it was only to look over the decree her attorney had drafted. For me it was really about the parenting plan, and we had gone over that with a fine-toothed comb.

The basis of that parenting plan was built on the old model of parenting. Dad = breadwinner, Mom = love and nurture. That was simply not true for us. And it is not true now. But now, my kids are in seventh and ninth grades, and the time with them is much more sparse and rational. My then-wife and my fancy divorce therapist sold me the old party line about Dads and Moms in divorce. I hope that if you are in this situation, you consult a lawyer who can negotiate on your behalf. If you parented 50/50, you should divorce 50/50 as well. The traditional divorce schedules and laws established when my parents were fighting it out no longer apply for most families.

18.

The Three Immutable Laws of Positive Co-Parenting

You have to release them both, your kids and your ex, and let them fly.

My ex-wife and I don't see eye to eye on a lot of things. But one thing we've kept relatively clear over the last five years of divorce is THE KIDS COME FIRST. Always.

We've had issues between us, and I think two people in a relationship will always have issues, but we've kept them out of our parental relationships. So many divorces before us, I've seen angry divorced moms trashing their former partner in front of her two kids while waiting on the school bus together. And the incidence of Parental Alienation Syndrome (PAS) is also real. I can't imagine using your kids as a chess piece to get back at your former spouse. Yikes.

But when you've agreed to disagree over things like money and custodial versus non-custodial role, you can still agree to keep the kids clear of any of the disagreements between you. In our case, we used a divorce therapist to help us split the baby, so to speak. And in her office we could talk about things like "in the best interest of the children" while still arguing about our own wants and needs. It's not about what's fair, at that point. It's about what situation would support the kids.

Right, the goal of "less disruption for the kids at this difficult time" was hard to me to argue with. And in typical fashion I was shown the door, given a less-than status and a substantial child support payment, and I said "thank you" at the end of it. Even today, I'm not happy about the current parenting schedule and financial burden I've been given, but I'm not fighting about it, either.

Today, "in the best interest of the kids" means something very different than it did five years ago. Today my kids are 13 and 15. They have their own agendas. And we all find our way forward with as little conflict as possible, both the kids and their mom. Even while there are some big issues and big questions in the legal and financial part of our relationship, the devotion to the kids and their conflict-free childhood remains our guiding principal.

At the core of it, I know we are both doing the best we can. Giving her the benefit of the doubt, even when I'm mad as hell at her, is the only route. And making sure my issues are cleared up before I am with my kids, that is my responsibility.

How easy it would be to spout off the, "Well, your mom..." But we don't. At least I don't think she does, as it's never gotten back to me about any snarks about our situation. And we've been through some tough scrapes. Money has occasionally been an issue for both of us. "Somehow we just keep working it out. We will get there," she wrote to me in a text message.

And you can tell how well you are doing by your kids' energy and enthusiasm. In the first few years, things were a bit moody with all of us. But even in that hard slurry of depression, we, the four of us, kept encouraging each other, in spite of, and through, the hard parts. That's what we are now. Cheerleaders. We've got other responsibilities too, like leadership, morals, and guiding them towards a happy career path, but mostly, at this age, we have the role of cheerleader.

And in some ways, I'm also a cheerleader for their mom's

success. In her two-and-a-half-year relationship, regardless of my feelings about the guy, I have to cheer them on. My daughter likes him. And my ex-wife seems a bit more relaxed since they've been together. So, sure, I can be a "rah rah" co-parent for them. I'm glad my kids have another adult who cares about their welfare. And he's a good influence on all three of them.

When your partner's partner comes to your daughter's volleyball game at the end of a workday, you've got to give kudos. I'd be just as easy to "work late." But he shows up. And they sit together. And my daughter makes sure she hugs and says goodbye to both of them. That's a WIN WIN. A win for my daughter. And a win for my ex-wife.

Let's find the win in our divorces. Even before we've found a win, or a relationship in our lives, it's important to show our kids how well we still support and champion the other parent.

A reader sent me an email about one of my posts. She was concerned that I was going to share my ex-wife's transgressions with my kids. I responded about why I'm writing this blog: "No, it's important for me to know that eventually the whole story will be told. But today, it's all about positive parenting for me. If they read the book of the divorce in five or ten years, when they are adults themselves, that's fine, but that's not my intention."

Divorce is a bitch. And compartmentalizing your anger and sadness is a difficult process, but an essential one.

She replied, "That's great to hear, because my parents were real assholes to each other after the divorce. And all it did was make me and my siblings want to get as far away from them as possible when we left the house. None of us are close with my parents."

There's the crux. Attachment parenting is about letting your kids know, from the moment they are born and for as long as they live, that they are loved and supported regardless of their choices. And in divorce you have to keep that objective in mind. If you attack or belittle their other parent, you are breaking one of the fundamental rules of co-parenting.

The 3 immutable laws of positive co-parenting:

    1. 100% positive

    2. Kids first

    3. Honest feelings

From that position of strength and cooperation, we can manage anything, together, both the kids and my ex-wife and her boyfriend. And my girlfriend, too. (grin)

If you can remember the flight and joy of your children as the goal, you can forgive, forget, and move on from nearly any personal issue or frustration with your ex-partner. That's your responsibility, not your kids' or your ex-partner's. You have to release them both, your kids and your ex, and let them fly.

IV

What Dating Looks Like Today

Tinder, Facebook, OkCupid, the options are unlimited. And somehow it's harder than ever to find an honest to goodness wholesome date. Most dads aren't trolling the internet looking for a partner. If he's too busy to date, or to plan dates, you might have to make it easier for both of you. You've got kids, he's got kids, how do you sync the schedule?

19.

Action, Not Intention, Will Determine How Long I'm Single

> Single moms are sexy. And if they play tennis... well... I'm getting the picture.

Relationships are a force of nature. When we don't have them, we suffer from loneliness, boredom, ennui. When we do have them, we suffer from feeling smothered, codependent, and overwhelmed. And of course, there's the up side. When you're single, the options are limitless. You've got online dating sites, apps like Tinder, and all the potential dates you could imagine. And a lot of free time to spend searching, buffing yourself up, and putting your best foot forward.

As I begin the conscious move away from online dating and into real-time dating, I'm aware that it takes a lot more energy to actually go out. In truth, we get lazy. We think that browsing online profiles is kind of like dating. We tell ourselves we're upping the odds by adding our own hopes and wishes to the online pool of potential partners. But mostly, for me, I'm understanding that I'm lazy. The effort is 100% up to me. And some nights, even when there's a known woman at a known event, I skip it. I'm understanding more about what's going on when I opt-out in the real world.

- Online dating (the browsing and contacting part) is

easy. There's very little risk. It takes very little energy. And, in theory, you are browsing hundreds of available women in your area.

- Online profiles cannot translate any of the feeling part that you get when you're in proximity with another person. When there's a spark, you can feel it, before anyone has spoken. Without it, well… you've just wasted an evening and several dollars trying to find out.

- Even great pictures AND great texts or emails don't equal a match. I'm learning to reel it back in a few notches. I used to engage in long romantic chats with potential women only to be sadly disappointed when we finally met.

- The lack of energy required to "date" online is equal to the energy you are going to get back. Feeling lazy, too lazy to go out? No problem, whip up OkCupid and cruise the internet a bit.

So what are some of the things that make putting yourself out there in the real world more challenging? What are the things that keep me at home on a Sunday morning, when I know there's a spiritual service nearby that is likely to include several attractive single women?

- I'm not feeling too great about myself. This can be energetic, spiritual, or physical.
- I just don't have the energy to put my A-game together.
- I'd rather do something else.

- I'm afraid of rejection or looking like a fool.
- I'm just a little bit comfortable in my aloneness.

But in several years of seeking, I can tell you that a love poem is never going to get the girl. It might get someone interested. It might even illicit an email when it's published online. But it's only the intention without the action. It's the romantic longing for romance without the risk. It's not easy to get excited by someone and be let down by their lack of resonance.

I was just looking back over a near-miss from a few years back. The woman in question had popped up on OkCupid again. She still looked as delicious as she did. Well, she's using the same profile and the same pictures, so of course, she looked good. And she reminded me of how I can imagine everything is ON when it's not. What she showed me, for the first time since my divorce, was dating and finding the right combo of looks, intelligence, and joy, is tough. It's not as easy as flipping through some profiles, having a nice hello and... even after two hours of inspired conversation... it's still a NO?

Okay, so what's different for me now? What needs to be different for me to find my next relationship, not date. I know what I have to do.

- Focus on myself.
- Be radiant and potent in my walk through the world.
- Get fit because I deserve to be stronger, healthier, and more energetic.
- Go out even when I don't feel like it.

I was in a cardio workout with two very attractive women. I was noticing my own joy at just being around them. I did not have any designs on them. I did not proposition either one of them. And the banter during the workout was hilarious and untethered to any idea of "dating" or romance. Oh, I guess I should mention, they were both married. BUT... two weeks ago, when the same two women were in the cardio class with me, I'm certain that the "friend" was not wearing her ring. Certain antennae perked up in my brain and I noticed how I took her in with slightly different eyes, imagining that she was a single mom.

Single moms are sexy. And if they play tennis... well... I'm getting the picture.

Parenting is a life journey that I've committed myself to. My partner should have the same orientation. And tennis, being my favorite sport, is a passion that if shared, can unlock a lot of positive feelings and shared time together.

New direction. I must find a partner for the mixed doubles league. So I took a step in that direction. I asked one of the two women if she knew of anyone who would be interested in joining a mixed ladder as a team.

She smiled and asked, "Would you prefer a single woman?" The banter between us was rich.

"Well, that would be a double win, but not necessary." Then she delivered the kicker.

"I'd do it, if I didn't already have so many commitments. But I'll give it some thought."

Just those two little ideas generated a nice warm fuzzy inside of me. She would... She'd think about it on my behalf. And because I know we already get along (this woman has been coming to the cardio class for months), I could imagine that she would. And of course, she does have a lot of women friends who also happen to play tennis. And maybe who happen to be single. Who knows. It's not about her or her friends, it's about the intention, the idea, and the action.

NEW Dating Goal: I will take specific actions to meet single women who play tennis. WIN WIN.

20.

Offline Dating: Setting Intentions and Actions in Real Life

Let's start with an assumption: you are looking for the next real relationship of your life. Now let's look at what's wrong with online dating.

- Primarily based on photos
- Photos can be retouched, enhanced, and from much earlier times.
- Most profiles begin to sound the same (long walks on foreign beaches, red wine, and having fun).
- Most of what you see in someone's profile is what you want to see.
- Many people are just playing on dating sites, just like Facebook; they're killing time.
- The "matches" are usually so far off, sites like eHarmony are actually depressing.
- Age is just a number.
- A lot of men and women lie about their age.
- There's no way to sense chemistry via an online profile, email, phone call, or text. (Phone calls do get close, but it's two-dimensional rather than three-

dimensional.)

Here are some myths about online dating that might be more marketing than reality.

- It ups your odds of finding the right person by making a lot more people available for dating.
- Many people have found the love of their lives using online dating sites.
- It's better than the bar scene.
- There are 1,202 women who match your search criteria.

Um, yeah, if there were that many women who were attractive, charming, smart, and had a creative passion in their lives, I'd already be married again. As it is, I'm not even dating. And the one person I dated from an online dating site WAS super, but she's one out of at least 45 dates and perhaps 1,000+ outreach requests I've put into the system.

So what are the alternatives to online dating? If I'm not going to browse and click my way into a new relationship, what's it going to take?

Here's what I think.

For me, chemistry is part sexual attraction and part magic. There is no way to get a hit of either of these things online. But when you experience them in real time, you know it immediately. With that understanding, several real-world criteria might help me find a relationship.

Spiritual but not religious. What this means to me is the person may or may not go to church, but her spiritual belief system is strong and vibrant in her life. With that essential element to my perfect mate, I can assume that she probably attends some of the following places: alternative churches in my city, yoga studios all over town.

Health conscious. I'm more likely to meet my next mate in a Whole Foods than in a McDonald's. I'm not sure how you go about meeting someone while shopping, but I guess if people are putting out the "hello" vibe, you can sense it. I need to be more observant, more conversational, more open to nuance and fresh produce.

Active lifestyle. (Tennis and trail walking are my two favorite pasttimes.) She's got a fitness program of her own, for sure, but wouldn't it be amazing if she also played tennis? What if I started there? What if I actually worked at networking through some of my tennis friends to find a mixed doubles partner? The first woman I dated since divorce, who played tennis, was a total turn-on when she smacked a top-spin forehand. Why wouldn't I want to do my favorite sport *with* someone? Okay, note to self: tennis networking = priority number 1.

Creative living. I went out on a couple of dates with a woman who kept repeating, "You're so creative." At first I thought it was a compliment, and I'm sure she meant it as a compliment. But what I started realizing was she was saying, "Wow, you are *so* creative. I am not very creative. I'm amazed by creative people." Oh. So, I think I need to be with another creative person. Because this writing and songwriting isn't going to happen unless I preserve some alone time. My perfect mate has to desire alone time as well and, when we come back together, has to be able to bring some of her creative energy.

Mind over body. I'm probably not going to get my six-pack abs back. I'm probably always going to have love handles. So I'm not looking for a body-builder girlfriend to admire and worship. What I know is my mate has to be happy in her own skin. If everything is about fitness and diet and beauty, then I'm going to be left behind. And probably a bit bored. We all need to work on our health and fitness, for life. We all need to live with as much vitality as possible. If fitness and working out give you that jolt, go for it. (I know tennis does it for me.) But let's hook up in our mental space as well. We've got to spend a lot more time talking than lovemaking.

In joy. Happiness is not something you can buy or learn. (Though you can work on it.) Happiness is the feeling you get when you are around someone positive and hopeful. If I learned anything from my last marriage, it's that I am very hopeful and very positive, sometimes to a fault. But that's also the person I'm looking for. Someone who smiles more than frowns. Someone who wakes up each morning with wonderment and a stretch towards what's possible.

Intense and low key as needed. I am most jazzed when I'm performing. I do have Type A, driven characteristics, and when I'm ON, I push hard for what I want. But I also have a quiet repose, where I recharge and relax. I do want someone who can jolt up with me and climb the mountain. And then the next day uncoil on a beach for a day without any objectives or requirements. In contrast comes my power and pleasure. Let's spark one another and massage one another as needed, in the moment.

I cannot catch a glimpse of the above characteristics from an online dating profile. And sure, over time, over the course of a few dates, I could get there, but what if we just started in reality? What if we knew what we wanted and showed up at those places in those ways to be seen and to seek? That's the real-world method of communicating, and that's what I'm planning. This year, every time I get the inclination to open Match.com, I'm going to make a concrete plan to do something in the real world that will put me in contact with real women.

I'll let you know how it goes.

21.

Why Online Dating Is a Distraction and Not a Solution

Yes, I know the statistics. All the happily married couples from online dating sites. Well, I don't buy it. All online dating sites, regardless of the flavor or method, are more like Facebook than real life.

Here are a few examples of where online profiles don't tell the truth.

- Pictures lie. Even recent pictures, when taken with the right light, can make a NOT look like a HOT.
- Words are made-up ideas. Yadda yadda, we all like beaches and wine. Music maybe.
- Chemistry is impossible online. You can't imagine how that person will feel when you are together.
- The mind is wonderful, but even eloquent emails and text messages can add up to zero when you meet.
- Some people are on dating sites for the entertainment of the idea and not to date.

Yes, it is true, online dating sites increase your odds of meeting people you otherwise might never come in contact with. But why is that? Because you come in contact with people when you are out and about and doing the things that are important and fun to you. There's a reason that an extroverted creative type like me isn't going to naturally run across an introverted mathematician. It's because we have so little in common, virtually zero overlap. And while the idea of "getting to know someone" is intriguing, you've got to start with some common ground to establish a relationship.

So I'm bored on a weeknight and have some unscheduled time. I can choose between a lot of different activities. I could go out and get some exercise, that would be good. But barring the self-improvement regimen for a minute, I could (a) spend time on Facebook chatting about nothing, (b) spend time on Match.com browsing faces for a hit, or (c) do something creative. What I've come around to lately is that (c) is the only good answer. Let me explain.

Facebook seems like community. We call it social media, but it's becoming more just media media. They're showing you approximately 8% of your friend's status updates and messages. The rest… is Facebook. Pabulum. Media. Consumerism. Today Facebook is a lot more like TV than it used to be. After taking a 99-day break from my Facebook habit, I'm happier and more productive. I've dipped back in a little, but no more hours socializing.

Online dating may seem like a beneficial and worthy activity. But because of the illusion of social media, we might think we have a pretty good idea of who these "potentials" say they are, and what they look like today, but we don't. It's simply not true. Profiles on Facebook or OkCupid are very similar. You put your best pictures up, your best accomplishments, and your little quirks. Except on dating sites you don't get to see the quirks. (Well, OkCupid's questions sections are full of quirks, and kinks, but that's a different conversation altogether.)

Creative process is where I grow as a person and as an artist (writer, musician, poet, whatever). And as I am growing myself up and growing into my creative energy, I am also putting out more energy and more joy. You see, I think this dating thing is all about joy. It's a little bit about looks. And it's a little bit about thoughts. But the chemistry thing, I think, is all about mutual joy. Do you feel it when you are with someone or not? If you feel joy at the sight of someone, there's a hit. If you feel nothing or something less than nothing (negative), that's also an indicator of where things might go.

I spent a good part of a week getting to know a new woman recently, and I could see the potential. I could admire her good looks, dark eyes, and flashing wit. And yet there was something that was not coming across. I couldn't decipher it right away. I was hopeful and encouraged by our initial and mutual glow. And her persistence in getting back together again the next day. "Spontaneously." I loved that. "Yes, yes, yes," it said to my brain.

But...

In my joyous engagement I was missing something from her that I couldn't identify. I thought I was listening well, responding well, and behaving well. I thought we were moving things along nicely. But I could only make those assumptions about myself and my own thinking. While she was sharing a lot about life and asking a lot of questions about me, she wasn't really lighting up. She was reserved. She admitted to being an introvert. I initially thought, "Oh, that'll be interesting, to see how I am in relationship to an introvert."

And even in the real world, with all of our faculties between us, the miss between us was something deeper. And after three "dates" and the promise of an actual "date" for the weekend ahead, I was feeling good and yet still mixed. I walked away from our meeting wondering, "Am I pushing this one along? Am I making this one happen? Am I trying to construct my lover?"

I think I was. She pinged me the next morning saying she'd considered our time together and felt it wasn't going to be a match for her. She was canceling the date. And would catch up with me spontaneously as the occasion might arise in the future.

Huh?

I was feeling the miss on a deeper level, but I was trying to make it all right. I wanted "her" to work. And that's when I understood it was time to kill my online dating profiles. I WANT a relationship too much. My focus has gotten lost in all this browsing, assessing, and pursuit. What I really need to pursue is my dream and my creative output.

I have time for a relationship. I have the will and the energy. I need to put myself and my life in the places where "she" already is. In real life, not online.

Sure, I will have another great love. First, I must become the lover I hope to meet, by becoming large enough to call her in, without the help of a dating site.

22.

Getting Good at Blameless Breakups

If you've been dating again since your divorce, you've likely had a couple of relationships. (Relationship – *def*: a monogamous dating experience that lasts more than a few months.) And unless you are still in the relationship, you've also experienced a few breakups. Let's look at the fine art of breaking up well.

When you break up well, a few things go differently than you remember in your youth, perhaps.

- You're not bitter and angry with the ex.
- You don't stalk them virtually or in real life.
- A text from them does not automatically mean they are looking for a hookup or to give you a piece of their mind.
- The breakup is more about compatibility than "you done me wrong."
- You can walk away from the relationship without an extended recovery period.
- You might really believe the statement, "I hope we can eventually be friends."
- You actually do become cordial with your ex.
- Their Facebook connection remains in tact and you don't feel the impulse to check in on them.

And the ultimate indication that you broke up well:

- You are happy for them when they find another relationship. I mean really happy, and not the "dang it, why don't I have another relationship" kind of grimacing happy.

I can say that I'm "friendly" with my exgirlfriends. This ability to break up well indicates a good, healthy attitude about dating and relationships in general. It's important that you are okay with dating, checking things out, and not forming a relationship too quickly. It's part of the territory. If you date, you are going to break up. If you break up well, you can go into the next potential relationship with a positive and healthy attitude.

It's a lot like your divorce. If you're still spouting vitriol about your ex, you might need to have that looked at before you start courting new women. They are going to pick up on your negative vibe right away. And it's easy to spot a bitter person a mile away. Dating is the same way. If the drama is high, the bitterness and anger will tend to come out in any "So tell me about your recent relationships" discussion. It's an essential question and one that you should ask while paying close attention to their answer.

Bitter breakups cause a chain reaction.

- There is a mistrust from the beginning, because either one of you is afraid of being hurt again.
- The baggage from the previous relationship (breakup or divorce) still hangs heavy in the mind and will color the openness and joyful potential.
- It's not a long shot to imagine the few terse words for the previous ex will be brought to bear on you, should

you "do them wrong."

- Unfinished anger work comes out in present relationships.

You want to start the next relationship with a clean slate. The new partner is not evil but also does not possess the ability to fix/heal/transform you into a happy person again. The joy you bring into the next relationship is equal to the joy you have in your life. If you've got some of your resources tied up in bad mouthing your ex, or even if you don't talk about it but feel it, you're going to hold back in your next relationship.

Here's the test.

- Can you see the new person without any preconceived judgments about his or her motivations or intentions?
- Are you able to stay present when people are talking about themselves, or do you keep jumping forward into future "scenarios?"
- Does your heart genuinely open when you are with the other person? Or are you feeling protective and cautious?

It's not about getting it right 100% of the time. That's silly. Finding your next relationship is a matter of trial, error, and breaking up with the ones who don't work out. And until you find the next "real love," that's all of them. And if you're planning on the "date" to NOT be the one, you are going into the new relationship with a defensive attitude, one that will not show you in the best light.

Before entering into the next relationship, make sure you are clear of the last one. How healthy are you on a scale of 1 – 100? If you're anywhere below 90%, take a break. You'll just do more harm than good by trying to "date" before you're really clear on what you want. And as you enter a relationship with old baggage, you will end it with more baggage. The bad stuff seems to compound unless it's dealt with.

Here are some ideas for how to break up well next time. (This list assumes there was no egregious freak-out or infidelity on either partner's part, for that requires a lot more work when it happens.)

- Don't make it personal. Make it easy and simple. "It's just not working out."
- If you care about them, let them know that you do.
- Give some pause between the statements and let both of you have a say in you are feeling.
- If you think you can be their friend, tell them that. If you don't think you can be friends right away, let them know that as well. "I do think we will be friends eventually, but I can't be around you right now, while I'm processing this."
- And then wish them well in both word and in your heart. By giving them the benefit of the doubt and assuming that they are a good person who just needs a slightly different person, you can honestly wish them well.
- If drama begins to break into the conversation, either find a way to shut it down ("Can we not get into that right now?") or take a break and try again later. ("I'm sorry, this is too much for me right now. I need to go

now and come back to talk about this later.")

The goal is never to blame the other person for the breakup, even if they were the reason you are breaking up. Always take your responsibility for the miss. And make it about the chemistry, the mix, the overall relationship and not about them or their poor behavior. Remember, you are leaving the relationship, not trying to teach them a lesson or educate them.

If you can execute a blameless breakup, you can walk away as friends and hold your head high in search of your next positive experience: starting a relationship (and likely eventually ending it). If your goal is always to end well, you can start with the same positive outlook. Who knows, maybe that's the key to finding your next keeper.

23.

Ready or Not-Ready for a Relationship: The Dating Game

It's a game. People's profile pictures are 10 years old. Their profiles forget to mention they're not divorced yet. Or, the most insidious, they're simply not ready for a relationship. They are testing the waters, checking it out, seeing what's out there. Blah!

So what does ready for a relationship mean?

> 1. Not currently in a relationship
>
> 2. Sufficiently through with their emotional issues
>
> 3. Interested in spending time with someone besides their kids
>
> 4. Emotionally intelligent (expresses feelings, can listen without offering advice)
>
> 5. On the positive side of life (not looking to be rescued or to be a caretaker)

Dating is simple. Relationships are hard work. Well, they can be hard work, or they can be temporarily effortless. I think that's what we're imagining when we jump back into the dating pool again. We remember the highs of love crushes, the sex, the joy, the "hi, I am soooo glad to see you" feelings that are bantered back and forth when you are establishing a new love relationship.

But the R-word has some issues for many people. And I've run across my share of women running from any kind of commitment. Sure, that's one way to be. And perhaps, in the early stages of divorce, a light approach is better; you really don't need a relationship, you need a healing.

There are a few simple signs that a person is NOT ready for a relationship.

> 1. They are still bitter or angry about the divorce or their ex (until someone has moved on, it is very hard to be in a relationship).
>
> 2. Their profile just talks about "having fun," and all their pictures involve a glass of wine.
>
> 3. They can't stop talking.
>
> 4. They talk about their multiple lovers.
>
> 5. They've got no banter (they can talk about work, working out, and partying).
>
> 6. You get the feeling you are with someone who's still in college (fun is fine, but fun isn't everything).
>
> 7. Everything is superficial (if it's hard for them to tell their breakup story, perhaps they're not ready).

Here's what you want.

> 1. You find the person non-threateningly attractive.
>
> 2. They are optimistic and positive (I'm beginning to

think optimism is the trump card).

3. They can jump easily from divorce and dating conversations, to music, to whatever.

4. You get a happy feeling when you see them (this could be the definition of chemistry).

5. At the end of the first date, you are both signaling, "What's next?"

It's really that easy. A first date is a sniff test. Do I find the person attractive in real life? Are they open and interested in me too? Are they intelligent and optimistic? Do they have the time and energy to begin exploring a relationship?

Walking around the lake today with a friend, he mentioned, "I'm meeting a lot of women who are not at all interested in a relationship. They seem to just be playing around. Or they are aloof and distant."

What is it about our later stages that would keep us in a casual or uncommitted mode? Perhaps we're not done processing the past relationship. Or maybe our kids are the priority, but in a way that precludes any time for a relationship to be built.

There is no mystery about the time and effort it takes to build a relationship. If it's casual sex you're looking for, perhaps you can find it without much concern for the other person's immediate mental state, but that's a zero-sum game, if you are hoping to find and nurture a new relationship.

I've often said, "I'm not into dating a woman, unless there is long-term potential." And I think what I am saying is that without the features and opportunities for a lasting relationship, I'd rather not spend the time and effort to gain a new "friend." It's fine. It's a bit Type A. I get that. I could have a lot more friends at the moment, if I'd be willing to share my time with non-romantically inclined women. But I'm not.

If there's no kiss in the future, I'd rather move on to the next "potential."

You see, even though we've been given back all this time, as divorced adults, we've also got a lot of work to do to recapture our essence. It is not enough to survive again, we long to thrive. And if LOVE is not the greatest opportunity to thrive, I don't know what is.

I was lucky recently to get close. To find another person who said "yes." And then the old witch "timing" kicked in, and her life took off in a very unexpected and seemingly accidental direction. And that was that. All the earlier ingredients were present, the magic, the lust, the flirty anticipation... And then we were done.

I am happy for her, and we parted wishing each other the best of luck. But I was just about to feel what it was like when the other person, the other ATTRACTIVE person said "yes."

I'm still ready.

24.

Peaceful Easy Feeling: Looking for a Joyful Woman

I was eating breakfast at a Panera Bread this morning and I noticed a woman who came in and got in line. She was with her two kids and husband (I assume). And there was something about her… I couldn't quite put my finger on what the attraction was, but it felt familiar.

And a month ago I had a first "hello" date with a woman who was cheerful, full of life, and boisterously funny. Her wit and energy was infectious and almost a challenge. Like she was daring me to be boring or unentertaining.

I want that. I want some enthusiasm. It's what I bring, I know this. But I am ready to have some of it reflected back at me. And when you see it, when you notice the happy person in the room, something draws you in. The woman this morning wasn't stunningly beautiful or amazingly fit, but her vibrancy radiated out from her, even as she stood in line with her brood. There was nothing amazing about her or the moment, but there was "something."

What is the quality of joy? How do you quantify someone else's happiness?

In a simple online dating exchange today, a woman thanked me for the positive vibes. I had to check out her profile and see who she was and what she was talking about. I think I gave a thumbs up to one of her photos yesterday. (The most passive of "hellos.")

And then the banter was so easy and so simple between us that four emails later we made a date. It was easy. It was fun. It was different from most online dating interactions and very different from most interactions over all.

I've just pulled back from a relationship I was pretty stoked about. I was becoming more and more concerned with the "work" we were needing to do to maintain even our casual relationship. And what I noticed in this release is a re-commitment to "what I'm looking for." I'm not looking for a project, or even a work-in-progress. I'm looking for a fully alive and empowered woman who brings a joy with her. That joyful attitude is something you can feel. Even as I was aware that the woman this morning was married, I was fascinated by her radiant joy. How her life force, or something, some glow, was capable of nailing some happiness radar in my heart and letting me know, "HEY HERE IS ANOTHER HAPPY PERSON."

It's a bit like looking for your tribe. I've been a joy-generator for a long time. And I am looking now for my Joy Tribe. The happy people. The women who glow with something intangible but palpable. I could feel it, but I didn't understand it at first. And then my whimsical exchange with the online dating woman reminded me. It's playfulness, it's banter, is something easy about the flow of information and a building connection.

I don't have any real data about the woman I made a date with. And I should go back and examine her profile a bit closer, but… I'm okay on giving in to whimsy every now and then. Heaven knows my calculated strategy hasn't worked out so well so far.

I'm imagining the next relationship as something from the Joy Tribe. I want a woman who is full of herself and full of some extra little magic touch of joy. Let's start there.

25.

Five Myths and Five Truths About Online Dating Today

There is no such thing as online dating, unless you consider texting and emails a form of dating. The dating begins the moment you step into a coffee shop or wine bar together. Or, better for me, meet along the local walk/run trail and get acquainted without mind-altering beverages. So let's get rid of that one first.

Online Dating Myth 1: Online dating is not a form of dating. It is a means to an end. Offline dating is the goal.

Online Dating Truth 1: Some women will string you along, making it seem like they are interested, but they will never accept the offer of a meeting. This is due to one of three things.

> 1. They're really not interested but are afraid to hurt your feelings.
>
> 2. They are overwhelmed by the great offers, and you've been given a number and place in line for when they get back to you.
>
> 3. They are not ready to date.

Online Dating Myth 2: A cute profile pic = a cute date. I'm pretty sure this one cuts both ways. I'm amazed sometimes, even in a person's range of photos, how they mix in the youthful babe shots with the "here's what I look like today, at 45." So you get intrigued by the hot shot, and when they show up for the date, um, what…? When was that other picture taken? It happens. It's not pretty.

Online Dating Truth 2: Cute dudes are not always assholes, cute girls are not always stuck-up princesses. But from the lack of compassion in online dating, you'd never know. The woman who engaged in three weeks of "hey, what's happenings" to "you're kinda coming on like a stalker" after I emailed her the second time in a week… Well, those people you'd best not get started with, even if they are cuter than hell.

Online Dating Myth 3: If a woman (or man) is actually really cute and not a head case, she'd never be online dating anyway. We're busy, we're tired of bars and pickup lines. We'd prefer Facebook, where we can see what you're really like, with your friends, but you're not a friend yet. I have met several amazing people via online dating. Two of them are still close friends and Facebook cheerleaders. So there are good people trying online dating, you just have to uncover the right one for YOU.

Online Dating Truth 3: If you recognize a disconnect in their profile, or in something they message you, and you have doubts about their authenticity, RUN. There are a ton of liars in online dating. Some are there just to troll and have fun. Some want to send you dick pics. Some want to lure you off to a pay-per-view sight where they can show you the "real pics." "Don't worry," these porn saleswomen say, "registration is free." Oh, and look for the cutie who is 10-15 years younger than you with a search range of within 500 miles and an age range of 35 – 75. They are trolls or sales folks trying to game the system for financial gain.

Online Dating Myth 4: Their profile is close enough, maybe not perfect, but what the heck... If there's doubt in your mind, there is probably a disconnect larger than you can imagine. People are putting their best spin on everything. Often they are lying about some significant facts. Like the woman who confessed within the first 30 minutes of a hello date, "I'm not actually divorced yet. But we're separated." Um... NO. If you get the feeling something isn't quite right when looking at their profile, just pass on the in-person. Why waste your time and your money chit-chatting with someone who's not really interested in a relationship?

Online Dating Truth 4: Women get propositioned about 10-to-1 over men. No matter how cute you are. Ryan Seacrest wouldn't really get that many propositions because women would fear his good looks like the plague. Women of marginal beauty, on the other hand, are hit on constantly. Now, this isn't to say they are getting valid or polite propositions. And I would guess (since I'm not a cute female, I'd have to guess) that the cuter they are, the more careful they have learned to become. So the cutest girl on OkCupid is probably propositioned once ever 10 minutes, but she's still only got seven evenings a week. There's a great study from OkCupid about how good-looking people are perceived by their photos ("Your Looks and Your Inbox: How Men and Women Perceive Attractiveness," an OkCupid survey report by Christian Rudder).

Online Dating Myth 5: Chemistry can be sensed or determined by texting or emailing. No way, José! Forget about it. I can't tell you the number of times the chemistry was smokin' hot and their profile photos were awesome and the in-person meeting was a dud. Whatever you think you see, whatever magic you think you can sniff out through romantic projections and their flirtatious response, forget about it. In fact, save your energy for other things. Rather than build up the pre-in-person courtship, move on to getting some exercise or finishing that work project you've been procrastinating on. All that time and effort you put into wooing a woman online is nothing if you meet in person and something is off. There's no going back. You don't get your time back. Or your flight of fancy that kept you texting until 1:00 a.m. on a weeknight. Skip the romancing until you've established a mutual interest.

Online Dating Truth 5: Your first date may say, "Okay, see you again soon." There is a 50/50 chance that is a lie. Maybe greater. If there's no magic, a casual "Thanks, call me" is as bad as "Um, thanks anyway, but no." The problem is, it's much more misleading. Do everyone a favor. If there's no chemistry, and you're absolutely NOT interested in a second date, don't act like you are. I've had my just warming heart broken a couple of times by women who seemed to give a semi-warm "Sure, call me" and then turned out to be "not so much." Why didn't they just tell me? Even ending all email or text responses is a better answer than saying there's some interest when you know there isn't any. I know it's hard, letting people down. BUT DO IT. We're trying online dating to cut to the chase a bit. Don't prolong the misery by giving false positives.

I hope you meet a lot of nice people out there. But don't be fooled by their looks, their profile statements, or their fluent email banter. Go for the face-to-face meeting with as little hassle and energy as possible. If it becomes difficult to land the date, for whatever reason, move on. If they wanted to meet, they would also be trying to make it happen, not giving excuses.

And remember it's not online dating we're after. It's the dating that happens offline that is the real stuff. Good luck.

26.

A Sprinter in Love and How I Am Learning to Pace Myself

I was a sprinter in high school. After my years of playing football and lifting weights, I was a bit of a jock. And when I joined the swim team, I quickly learned that all those muscles were great for going fast but not so great for going the distance. I swam the 50- and 100-yard races of all strokes. I did okay, but I didn't set any records. But I hated swim practice where we would swim swim swim for an hour or so… UGH. I often felt like I was going to drown.

In my adult life I have become less of a sprinter in my physical exercise, taking a more measured approach to my fitness and life way. Here's what I mean. People either run or they walk, for the most part. I walk. When I run, the sprinter brain kicks in and I start running faster. Trying to catch the runner in front of me. Trying to beat the runner ahead as we head up the long hill. When I run I tend to get anaerobic and drive myself too hard. Sort of the way I did when I was swimming. If I swam at my natural sprint-like pace, I'd never make it through a half hour of swim practice. I learned to dial it back, to breathe a lot more, and to go the distance.

In walking versus running, I've also learned a similar pattern for myself. I CAN run. And when I do, I notice more pain, more exhaustion, and longer recovery time the next day. So if I go out and run 2 miles instead of walking 3.5 miles, I might get the benefit of the higher cardio workout, but I'm going to be hard pressed to get back up and run again the next day. If I walk, I can walk day after day without any real recovery days, unless it's really hot. (Texas summer heat is mean business.)

So, for my life and my style of fitness and my age, I walk. And I walk happily. I'll walk every day if I can. If I ran, I'd probably work up to daily runs or at least every other day, but what's the point if my joints start aching and if I am damaging my long-term ability to play tennis, or even walk? There's no point in it.

I know there's a time thing for most people. And running takes a lot less time and can give you higher benefits. But that's just fine with me. I'll walk, thanks.

In my relationships I tend to approach things like a sprinter (or runner). And I'm tired of the long recovery periods. I've learned that going fast may feel exhilarating, but it might be a flaw in my strategy. If I walked more in my dating process, perhaps I would become less focused on one woman and be more comfortable casually dating a few at a time. (I'm personally not talking about sex, but that's okay if *you* are. I'm just talking about "getting to know you" dating.)

Here's what I learned as a serious dating relationship collapsed under the weight of our collective mismatch. I had put all of my eggs in her basket, and that tended to make me more focused on her than perhaps I should've been. I wanted her badly, and our courtship turned to passion in a few weeks. And that wasn't the problem.

I was the problem. I wanted to run, jump, swim into "what's next" with her. I learned, in the course of dating her, to taper my sprint a bit. Only a bit. I was always hungry for her. I wanted to devour and praise and massage her all the time. Of course, as single parents that wasn't really an option. So we traveled along together side by side, her running and me walking on the trail, but in the cadence of the relationship I kept sprinting ahead.

Time after time I would write a love poem and think, "Man this is a good one, I should share it." And inevitably this would lead to a freak-out. Okay, back to walking. And then I would get a second wind and sprint back to the front of the pack and send another mis-timed missive. Damn. I didn't learn very quickly that this was a running woman, but she wasn't ready to run with me into an "R" relationship.

Now I know. And I have more time alone again to reflect on my pattern. Walk, walk, walk, sprint. It's the sprint thing that I can do without, at least in terms of dating. In my physical exercise I am happy to get some running in on the tennis court, THAT is worth it to me. But on the trail or on a treadmill? Forget about it.

So I know in my fitness, walking and walking frequently is the key to my happiness. It may be a longer haul to get as fit as I'd like to be, but I have very little pain and almost no need for recovery days. (Tennis in the Texas heat is a bit of a different story, but I try to play early in the morning when possible.)

Besides, if I ran I wouldn't have so much time to enjoy and study the music in my earbuds.

27.

Playdates for Adults: The Five Challenging Tasks of Finding a Partner

How to find play, fun, and love, maybe

This whole business of online dating has gotten too serious. We're way too focused on Type A goals.

- Find a date.
- Arrange an in-person meeting.
- Assess the "relationship" quality of the person.
- Pass, fail, repeat.

But love, or looking for a real relationship, is not really a Type A task. In the driven mode of dating we get criteria like these:

- Has (or doesn't have) children.
- Wants more (or doesn't want any) children.
- Is Christian, or whatever "spiritual but not religious" means.
- Would sleep with someone on the first date, given the right circumstances. Or wouldn't consider sleeping with someone until Dates 6-10.
- Is successful in business and likes travel to exotic

locations. Or still working for a living.

- Partier (most pictures have drink in hand) or "social drinker" or "doesn't drink at all."
- Has a rockin' bod. Or not.

Whereas these are some valid criteria, they are more for sorting through the cattle call of online dating profiles, rather than looking for a relationship. In a word, they are a bit superficial.

So some alternatives to online dating are worth looking at, if you are seeking a mate. Or perhaps even a one-night stand, if that's your thing.

- Meet-up groups
- Activity groups
- Spiritually related groups
- Workout groups

When you think about the person you might like to be spending your Saturday afternoon and Saturday night with, where do you imagine you might be on any given Saturday afternoon? It's your opportunity/responsibility to get yourself there. That other person might already be there. If you know the types of activities you'd like to be doing with another person, then get yourself to those activities as a single person and see if there are any other singles there.

The first task of finding a partner is showing up.

For example. if you were recently excited by the World Cup, you might have found a public place to go view the game. You might have stayed home and watched it on your computer. And even if that is what you would've liked to do with a "special friend," it's not very likely that you are going to be introduced to them while in your pjs in your living room. Get out there.

The second task of finding a partner is brightening up your presence.

You want to be the brightest spark in the room. If you are happy with yourself and confident in your mission, you can walk into a room full of drinking soccer fans and still hold your own torch. If your torch (your self-love, self-confidence) is sputtering, perhaps that's a good place to put your attention. Get your game in order before going out looking for game.

The third task of finding a partner is learning how to be charming.

Listening is an art. Often the most confident people listen better than others. The ones who are always needing to tell stories, be brilliant, and obviously work too hard at being charming are often still trying to find their inner confidence. If you want to be heard, listen. It's the most powerful thing you can do in the opening "is there chemistry?" moments of a face-to-face meeting.

The fourth task of finding a partner is showing your enthusiasm by actions and not just words.

If you want a second date, say it. If you don't want a second date, say it. And if you BOTH want a second date, you won't need to be emailing each other later to see if there was "chemistry." Believe me, if there's chemistry, you will both be asking,

"What's next?" And the answer will sound like this: "What are you doing for dinner?" or "What are you doing tomorrow night, I've got tickets to…" If you have to ask, there's probably not a connection. If there is a connection, and you are BOTH actually wanting a relationship, you will both be asking for the next meeting.

So much of this process is figuring out who is playing games, who is really ready for something, and who is too damaged from a previous relationship to be available.

The final task of finding a partner is being brutally honest.

You don't want games. You don't want new drama. You want clarity, well-stated intention, and a clear communication style with this person you might actually be interested in. Anything less is a red flag.

If you feel it, say it. If you don't feel it, say that too. Then return to Task 1 and LISTEN. The more you listen, the more attractive you will seem to the other person.

And the final tip of romancing a potential mate: Say their name back to them, repeatedly, like a poem.

> John Brock: The sweetest sound in the human language is one's own name.

Good luck out there.

28.

Dating Part-Time: I Get it, it Is Hard to Make Time

I get it. It's hard to find the time to date. Even when you have opportunities and willing partners, sometimes it's just more of a hassle than going on your own. Let me share an example about my evening.

I'm invited to a cool house party for a musician friend who's going to perform. And I sort of have two potential "dates" for the evening, but… I'm not calling either one. What? Hard to get closer, hard to find another lover, if we're always going by ourselves. Let's examine.

My first choice would be the second "woman with potential" who has been renamed "the muse." After three months of courting on all available "every other Saturday nights," we never even shared a sexual kiss. It's okay. But having an aspirational relationship is one thing. Being in a relationship with someone who's not that interested in going further is another. And after her three-week vacation up East, she's been too busy to get together. Best to let that sleeping muse rest quietly in her own world. She was happy and self-sufficient before I came into the picture, and she'll be fine with or without me. She's still aspirational, but on an artistic plane rather than a relationship one. Okay.

My second choice would mark a fourth date with a woman from OkCupid. She's cute enough and smart enough. And we've hinted around sexual discussions enough to know that an opening could be available for that. But... she's not the person I'm looking for. And I guess she knows it. My several "wanna have lunch" texts, which were really about having lunch, have gone unanswered. I guess she senses the heat is on or I'd be more active.

There's even a third woman who came on pretty strong on OkCupid and has since then gone dark. I just opened the site to see what she's up to, and she's apparently blocked me or dropped off the site. Okay.

So, I could call one of the first two women. And make plans to have a drink and some food before the show. And get a little contact time with either of these lovely women. BUT, it's easier to not call them and go to the show alone. Maybe there will be a nice woman there to chat up.

So in the slice of time that is available outside of being a single parent and doing our work, there is some space for another person. But the more you get into the alone time, the harder it is to work to fill it with opportunities. So the time goes along, and we're alone, and it's okay.

I'm pretty sure this is the story with the muse. She's not had a long-term relationship for years and years. And her 16-year-old daughter needs her. But even she said, "I might be using her to keep from making time available to be in a relationship." The bigger tell was when she returned from a three-week hiatus and hasn't really made any effort to connect. Then again, neither have I.

I write the love poems to soothe myself. I improve my fitness to feel better about myself. And I am readying the live band show in two weeks to bring my full creative potency back into fruition.

And when she shows up, it won't have to be WORK. There

will be negotiations to find the slice of available time to be together, but it will be **an effort in mutual attraction.**

29.

Every Other Saturday Night

If you've got kids and you are divorced, you're most likely on an every-other weekend schedule like me. While it affords plenty of opportunities for self-improvement and creative endeavors, it's hell on dating. AND if your "date" is also divorced with children, chances are their schedule is exactly opposite from yours, if they're on the SPO prescribed by the state and enforced on 80% of Texas men, for example.

Okay, so you've got approximately two weekends a month to do as you please.

In trying to move a significant love interest forward, it is hard not to press for some commitment. Some indication that we are in a relationship. We've snuggled. We've hugged goodbye and had the occasional closed-mouth kiss. And then we're off to the static silence that is the rest of the week in a busy single parent's life. She has a 16-year-old daughter, and that entails a lot. AND… of course we are both hyper-committed parents. For me that runs a staggered schedule; for her, with the father no longer in the picture, it's 24/7 mothering.

So rather than asking for some sign, I'm looking at the time. There is not much time to be together. And the joining takes effort and intentionality on both of our parts to make it happen. Why do I need some profession, some major milestone (a passionate kiss, lovemaking) to confirm our relationship? Do I? It might just be my longing and desire for those things, rather than some insecurity.

In terms of my available weekend nights, this summer, I have two Saturday nights a month. (I take my kids Thursday and Friday during summer vacation.) And now, with a little imagination, I can establish "dates" on those two nights and make the most of what is available.

I kept thinking, "Well, she's really busy." But it's ME who has the time. And for real relaxed socialization, the weekend offers the most return. So Saturdays it is. Every other Saturday.

That's not a lot of time to get time together. And today, at this moment, I'm okay with that. I admit to getting restless and desirous and checking my OkCupid profile for any "visitors" who might look interesting. But, in general, I think this developing story serves me well.

> 1. I am busily working on my creative craft (writing, journaling, playing music).
>
> 2. I am reinvigorated in my fitness and slimming quest.
>
> 3. I have an engine of passion and longing in imagining "being" with her (and this serves the love poem and love song output quite well).
>
> 4. And with things still being OPEN, I have flexibility and opportunity to explore whatever whims happen to arrive.

TIME is what we need to figure out how compatible we are. TIME is what it takes, for me, to understand adoration and appreciation, apart from the drive to have SEX or be in a relationship. I want those things. BUT, I'm clear that my mistakes of the past will not foreshadow my next relationship commitment.

When I jump in, this next time, I intend to jump in feet first. Both times I fell head-first in love and married before some of the fundamental parts of the relationship mismatch had not been revealed. (Of course, with hindsight I can imagine I would've seen them, but I was blind with passionate love.)

It's enough right now to know someone is out there, someone I aspire to, someone I adore and appreciate for herself, AT THIS VERY MOMENT, without ever having passionately kissed. (I can say this today; tomorrow might be a different tune.) She is showing me what ADORATION looks like when it grows and moves slowly.

Sure, I'd really like for a woman to take a shine to me and light up like a Christmas tree. And maybe that will happen, maybe this pause and calm/steady snuggle artist is just what I need to prepare me for what's next.

And I can use every ounce of energy to improve MYSELF and MY VISION and continue to dig into the wacky meanderings of my mind and my past/future mistakes. Most of all, I can stay present.

All of this self-examination is fine if we don't ruminate on the past or future. I feel, today, as if this writing has allowed me to shed the pain and dysfunction of my divorce and explore my life as a happy single person, again. And Girlfriend Number 1 showed me that I know how to be open, honest, and truthful in relationships. She showed the way to what's next. It is my job to stay present and not rush into anything (for any reason) unhealthy.

TIME is my most valuable currency. When planning my two Saturday nights, I'd be wise to choose with intention.

V

After the First Kiss

You've become intimate, now what? Crossing the boundary into sex prematurely can spoil the growth of a healthy relationship. If you really like him, wait a bit before jumping in the sack. Sleeping together means something today, just make sure you both think it means the same thing. Don't get entangled in a bad relationship just because you want sex. How do you take things deeper after sex?

30.

Sex Rules: The Frequency, the Fun, and the Fantasy

A couple of data points recently have led to me to contemplate what I know about sex and the differences between men and women. Let's see if any of this sounds familiar.

First, I picked up a book in the library called *Kiss and Tell: Secrets of Sexual Desire From Women 15 to 97*. I jumped quickly to the Cliffs Notes section and I read something I had suspected but could now confirm. There were no data given or study cited, but the message was very clear. Men (testosterone driven) crave sex all the time, it's part of our animal. Women (0.10 of the testosterone) don't crave sex in the same way and often require much more enticement to even think about sex.

Okay, so that's not all that new, but this next part was the confirmation I had experienced in my first two marriages. During courtship it is important to get to know your partner's level of desire. See, in the early phases of a relationship a woman's libido and testosterone levels are boosted by the novelty and excitement of sex. After several months in a relationship, assuming monogamy, the woman's sexual desire levels falls back to her normal level. The advice, from this woman and women's sexuality expert, was to figure that out early. If the two levels of desire are wildly out of sync, there might be a problem as the routine of sex becomes more predictable.

It's no mystery that women desire sex too. But what was news (at least confirmed my thinking) was that during the initial blush of a relationship your partner may exhibit sexual tendencies and enthusiasm that are not in line with her normal levels of arousal and desire. According to this expert, the range of normal sexual desire ranges from once a month, to once a week, to once a day. All of them being considered different but normal. No wonder the online dating questions about your sexual desire and frequency are so interesting and HELLO: IMPORTANT.

Second, I read a Dear Abby column about a woman talking about her husband's obsession with frequency of sex. Her mate of 30 years liked to track their sex on a spreadsheet and aim for 100 times a year. "Last year, we only had sex 72 times and he was upset."

Holy cow! 72 times a year is A LOT. About what I would LIKE, but expect? No way.

And Abby responded quite simply, he should stop acting like a college kid making marks on his bedpost and consider the quality of the sex and not just the frequency.

This got me to thinking about the discrepancy in my second marriage that began to show up more dramatically after our second child was born. When we were trying to conceive, the sex was wet, spontaneous, and playful. She had a bit more purpose and calculation than I did, but it was great. For some GOAL, her libido had risen to match the task.

Things started taking a nose dive at some point after our second child was born. It appeared that a comfortable frequency for my then-wife would've been once or twice a month. But letting a few months go by without accepting my offers of a massage or straight out asking to make love seemed like no problem to her. I tried to be a good sport and roll with it. But it was hard to make do with my hands and porn when I was sleeping next to a woman who I adored.

A few years after my daughter was born, I got a vasectomy. It seemed like a good thing to do, and I imagined we were both hopeful that it might provide some juice to our lovemaking attempts. Certainly not having to worry about protection was a big incentive.

And a funny thing happened that surprised both of us and reminded me today of the Dear Abby column. You see, when you have a vasectomy, the prescription is to have 45 ejaculations before coming back to the doctor's office to get tested for swimmers.

Woo hoo!

Somehow the GOAL really inspired my then-wife. It was like checking boxes on a spreadsheet or getting As on a test. We had sex all over the place. And it was occasionally just about getting me off and getting another gold star for the week. Fine with me.

We reached the goal, and suddenly we were able to have unprotected sex again. And things were HOT HOT HOT. For about a week. I'm not kidding.

We never recovered our sexual sync. And it wasn't too much later that things started to go off the rails on deeper issues. But I think it was indicated by my then-wife's return to an almost frigid libido. Again, I found myself making love alone rather than to a woman whom I adored and found to be my sexual ideal, in all except desire or frequency.

Keeping sexual communication open throughout the entire relationship is critical. As one partner starts closing off, and not just having periods of low sexual desire but shutting down the idea of sex, something is going to break down. And it's either going to be your relationship or your relationship to sex and how you connect with each other.

31.

Seeking, Finding, and Gifting the Spark of Love

It's a fragile thing, this spark we are all looking for. But it's essential for success in relationship, I think.

So this "spark" we are seeking in love, it's hard to find. And when we do find it, it's even harder to keep. It's easy to mistake sex or chemistry for spark. They are not the same thing.

The key to spark, however, is more than discovery. The key to spark, and sparking with others, is how they carry and care for your spark once you've revealed it to them. You see, I think we're hoping to GIVE our spark to someone for safe keeping and nurturing. We want someone else to see, love, and protect our spark. That little thing inside of ourselves we are proud of no matter what.

When you begin to wield your spark, many things happen. The other people interested in fire begin to show up.

In the last few days an amazing thing happened that helped me illuminate, for myself, a bit more about this concept of spark and what it IS and what it IS NOT.

I'll take them one by one.

1. Kissing Girl imploded. In the process of telling her my spark had dimmed in relationship to being with her, she bargained, she negotiated, she got mad. Kinda the stages of letting go, right? Anyway, what I saw in that change was how accurate this spark and spark awareness was for me. The minute I felt

the spark was not in the right place, I brought it back home to myself, and the proverbial floodgates of confused communications began. She blew up my phone with texts and calls within 15 minutes of a potential agreed-upon contact time. I can't abide that. Sorry. You and your drama must go.

2. The woman of the poetic and aspirational heart did a bit of a disappearing act. Not in action, but in presence, she became unavailable. A visiting friend, and then a scheduling conflict, and then, "Have a great weekend with your kids." It was only Wednesday. Easy handling here. No worries. No fear. We are still in the very early stages of "what if." I have not given her any of my spark. I have begun nurturing a spark for her, but that is all. I'm saving the poetry for a future time. At the moment it is a projection of my spark onto something that might not be accurate. So we breathe and relax. "Yes, have a good weekend."

3. The third woman texted and called me last night. It was a nice phone call. She was asking if I was available to join her for an event on Friday. I couldn't go. But I was happy to express how willing I would be in the future for similar invites. And I was clear that I was happy to hear from her. It was a warm fuzzy. She had reached back to me. After a moment of pause. Again, she's got spark potential, but it's still undeveloped.

What we want is someone who lights up when they see our spark. And then we want to be lit up by their spark as well. When we are together, our sparks have the potential to become a fire. But the process of bringing them together and being vulnerable and protective at the same time is something new and different for most of us.

I learned in my marriage to ex-y that passion and beauty can blow right over the spark. In the fits of desire, my own need, and my infatuation with her, I forgot, or missed, some core fundamentals that I should not have. No regrets. I have two beautiful children, and we soldier on as co-parents rather than parents. BUT... we could've had it all.

In fact, we did have it all. At least, I thought we did. And while she was carrying my spark I didn't even look at other women with the same eyes. I was DONE. I was HOME. I was COMPLETE. I was also misguided. But that's a story I've already told here.

So in the current moment, I am well aware of my spark and the sparks building with two potentials. How fun. And what I hope to learn, before moving too quickly with either of them, is how well our sparks fit together. How well we resonate, even in these very early stages. How easily does change get accepted, and how stressful are the resets? We are in this next journey for the big finish. (That's an idealistic concept, I know, but it's an intention and not a truth.)

So let's be sparking together. Let's see if we like the feel of the other person's personal flame. How can we support and champion their ideas?

Oh, and I almost forgot. I've killed my online dating profiles. Not in response to any of the above changes, but more in an attempt to simplify and be quiet. AND in that process, one final spark, OkCupid girl and I exchanged contact info. We'd been chatting on OkCupid for over a month. She was busy. I was easy. We were just being casual friends on OkCupid. But she was the only remaining spark. So I gave her a final ping with my email and cell number. And guess what? She texted me last night. And we had a funny exchange. And we'll probably go have a drink soon.

That's another learning. Hold on loosely. I learned this in spades with Kissing Girl. When they are TOO ready to engage or schedule, that might be a sign that something is missing in their lives.

And final thought. When you are aware of your spark, you can bring it to bear on a given relationship in a new way. As I am learning how precious my energy is, I am also aware that people of the fire are drawn to sparks. Unfortunately, so are the vampires. So as you bring your energy online and put the spark on your sleeve a bit more, beware of the baddies as well as the potential mates.

We're all learning this together. Today I spark. And voila, I have three potential sparkmates again. Like moths to a flame. Let's see who circles without imploding, getting burned, or lighting up too quickly. And I will be listening for their sparks. What songs are they singing about themselves and their lives? And how does their flame make me feel?

32.

Here and Now: Touching Objects of Desire

She's talking and I can't stop looking at her neck.

One of the women with potential is on the phone with me now and she's talking talking talking about how much help she needs and how she doesn't have time to get her stuff done. And she's talking and talking. And I'm not that interested in what she's talking about. All this talking, no necking.

The OkCupid woman and I had lunch yesterday and I was watching her neck. I had a longing, as if I were a vampire watching the pulsing of her life. I could imagine the same pulsing when we were making love; this is the throat of orgiastic pleasure. She's the one who sent me this text the day after we met for dinner:

> "Last night was fun, but I thought you were going to kiss me. What gives?"

I want to stop talking at some point. I want to be with someone and not have to talk about it. All the fking time.

There's some talking that needs to happen, some goals and rules that need to be established. But if there's no desire to kiss, it might be that there is very little kissing desire inside the person.

Case in point. I was with the OTHER woman of potential on Friday, during a window when both kids were away at friends' houses, and we just hung out. But she was warm and touchable.

She was close. She had cuddly all over her. Still no need to push in for kissing with her, but there was an implied closeness already. There was already touching.

If there's no touching, it's because TOUCH MIGHT NOT BE THEIR LOVE LANGUAGE, DUMMY.

Oh.

And the fact that the first woman with potential really needs me to help her with a lot of techie stuff... Well, it's starting to make me a bit tired. If it weren't someone I already knew, and if she hadn't been making the connection effort (she is), then she'd be a goner.

As it is, I'm already cooling a bit on her prospects. She REALLY reminds me of my ex-y. Things need to be just right, or fit some perfect form, or comply to her schedule and will... Nope. Not gonna do that again.

So I'm not cutting her off. But I'm beginning to expand my viewpoint again. And what if this new OkCupid woman was a kisser and then nothing? Well, that's okay. I'm chilling a little on the rule of only 100% or it's a waste of time.

The OkCupid woman is not an artist. She's very much into her gym and running. And she's cute as the devil and really easy to be with. So what if she's just a cute and easy, nice girl? Do they HAVE to be writers? Do they HAVE to share cerebral gymnastics or linguistic karate?

I'm fascinated with the shape and vibrancy of her neck while she's talking. We're exchanging stories about exes and parents. And when we get the check, she asks if she can pay. She's made it quite clear that she makes good money and is happy supporting herself and her two dogs. And all I can think about is how it would feel to make her neck strain with excitement. I'm hungry, but we've just eaten. It's a good feeling.

And she's cute as a button. Cute. Fresh. Easy. And she's asking me to kiss her. Except not in broad daylight. "It's gonna have to be a night date," she said, half seriously. She also had let me know, after the text above, that we would NOT be kissing in a restaurant or any other type of PDA. She simply wasn't into it. Okay, that's fine. But she asked me, "But dude, wth? Thought you were gonna kiss me but you didn't."

She's moving things forward nicely.

33.

Finding Adoration

Bringing sex into the picture can really complicate things. And when it's an animal drive rather than a move of adoration, it's something else. I'm not looking for animal sex with someone I don't crave. I want to make love, the next time, to someone I simply adore. That's the highest form of connection and adoration I can give. And I want to feel the loop going both ways. Like a circuit, a connection lights up both people.

I was listening to a Doyle Bramhall II song in the car today when the lyric hit me.

> You and me, we'll wait to see the day come down.
> Don't go, sit here girl, let's have a drink and watch the day come down.

Something about the longing in his voice and knowing that this record was a victory lap on his marriage to Lisa Melvoin (of Wendy and Lisa fame) just struck me as appropriate. I want to watch the day go down with a woman, just be. Time together being relaxed and not pressured to do anything.

And then I imagine the sex becomes part of the passion and adoration that grows between us.

It seems to me, I've been trying to hard to FIND a girlfriend. And what I learned yesterday, having a couple of hours hanging with the missing-in-action woman with potential, was this: it really is about the quality of the time together. The feeling you get. The unstoppable glow that wants to be fulfilled through the ultimate act of intimacy.

Sex is a spiritual act. And engaging in it should be a form of beauty and expression. When it becomes mechanical, or there's a hint of boredom or duty, it's done. I aspire to actually make love next time I'm with a woman. And until then, "friends" are just fine. Now, kissing... That's a bit less intimate and should be an indicator of the sensuousness in the relationship. But the intention should be there as well. So woman with potential might be overthinking, or she might just be really spiritual and going slow.

100% or just don't waste your time.

34.

Learning About Sex and Dating as We Go Along

I learned a couple of things yesterday that turned a light on in my brain. In the spirit of self-examination, and self-deprecating humor, I thought I would share and illuminate them for you as well.

Learning 1: Dating is not marriage.

In fact, dating (which I admittedly don't know much about) can be shut down by getting too serious or too future-plans oriented. As my schedule and future are quite flexible, I was surprised how quickly my "relationship" concepts changed yesterday when confronted with a challenging dilemma. On one hand I had met and "dated" an amazing woman. One the other she was telling me how our closeness and chemistry were freaking her out. And my reaction to the fourth letter in a series of Dear John letters was to accept her appraisal that we weren't really all that well matched.

Perhaps I just wasn't listening, I thought. She was trying to be clear with me, we were not really a match, and she was in no way ready to be a couple. Wait, what? "Okay," I responded. "I am disappointed, but I will accept your judgement." And that night I went to sleep saddened that I had missed or lost an opportunity for growth and maybe some more great sex.

I'm not sure what I dreamed about, but I know my inspiration was a lot lower when I woke up the next morning. And even after two cups of coffee, the bright enthusiasm was not returning. How close do we have to get in the early stages of a "relationship?" (Oh, the R-word.) What if we just kept it casual and "dated?" But wait, hadn't I just stated that the "long-term potential was critical to my plans" in a previous post? Hadn't I just sent her my Dating a Single Dad blog post?

I was imagining giving her a quick exit. Another one of my strategies when given a less than enthusiastic response has been to withdraw all energy towards that person and use that momentum towards some creative project or goal. So I was initially quiet when she texted me a nice "You're great, it's not you" message. I took the confused feelings and dug into my writing for the entire day.

But something stuck in my heart. Something didn't feel right. I was not the cold type to just freeze someone out, when the spark and energy had been SO right. By 10:00 p.m. my resolve or strategy was cast aside and I texted back.

> "You did not do anything wrong. I'm not mad, I'm disappointed. You too were great. Namaste."

Then I headed back off to dreamland, at least feeling like I had proposed the repair that might mean friendship, even if my heart would be at further risk of attachment.

Again some transformative sleep brought another level of acceptance and peace, so that when she suggested playing tennis the following day, I was excited and open to the idea. I measured my response and checked in with my heart. I would keep it within renewed boundaries. If I didn't venture my heart, perhaps I wouldn't be so dependent on her response.

Learning 2: 90% of our relationship hangups and aspirations are in our heads, and perhaps it's okay for most of them to stay there.

See, as I was professing "going slow" and "openness to whatever," I was ramping up my activity in a way that said, "Let's do this! Let's be together. Let me be a step-dad to your son, I'm a great role model."

STOP!

Even that was too far for me. My imagination, my internal romantic clock had gotten off, and I was shooting way ahead of our relationship and knowledge of each other.

Learning 3: Stay in the present.

When you get ahead of yourself, you tend to idolize or catastrophize in your visions of the future. And the future is NOT where it's at. It's about being open and honest with the time you spend together and learning what works and what doesn't.

In my past, jumping too far into the WE was disastrous. And this moment was no different. But now, we had no driving desire to make plans, only driving DESIRE. It's important not to confuse desire with love or marriage. Desire is critical to the success of a relationship, but the R comes a lot later.

I don't have much experience in dating post-divorce. The game has changed, and my intentions and priorities have changed. I am full of contradictions. That's okay. I may profess that I'm only interested in a Relationship while also saying I'm all about going slow. While the two things aren't mutually exclusive, they do present internal conflicts rather frequently.

But I am also a learning individual. I can adapt and make changes in my plans and trajectories. So while I was thinking I had lost orbit and was shooting away for some new destination, I might have been only slowing to the gravitational pull of this amazing lady and learning what her fears and passions were as well. By trying to adhere to some map I had of what I wanted, I risked another journey into the dark aloneness of outer space.

Today we played tennis. That's enough.

My new mantra: Reset, review, and repeat what works. Stay present.

35.

Unlocking Touch - The Love Language I Speak

If you buy into *The 5 Love Languages* (by Gary Chapman), then it's important to understand your language. Once you do, things can become a whole lot easier. Sure, you *can* be in a relationship with someone who has a different love language orientation, but it's always going to be a compromise between the two of you, reaching across your own needs to meet the needs of your partner. That's okay, but if you don't understand what's happening, it could be quite confusing.

I am clear on my love language. I speak touch. And once I own this, I can understand that most of my feelings of connectedness and caring come from some form of actual physical touch. I think of it sort of like a dog or a cat. When they want to be close to you, they actually get on you (cat) or they lie down against you. I'm like that. If we're within arm's reach, I'm usually going to reach out and give you a casual brush that says, "Hi, I care about you, I'm here." That's it. There's not really any sexual drive behind my need to touch. But there it is. I enter a room and see my kids or my significant other, and I want to touch them as a form of greeting, again a bit like an animal.

In my marriage, in the early days, we didn't have the love languages universe to compare notes. We entered into our courtship and eventual love with no meta-understanding of how we as individuals experienced feelings of love. We knew the usual suspects, time, attention, happiness, and compatibility. And of course, sex. But the nuance of what made us tick as a couple was still pretty hidden in our subconsciousness.

As we moved forward in our marriage and became parents with a mortgage in a nice neighborhood, and we succumbed to the stresses and trials of growing a family, we began to show signs of distress. And this is where our different love language DNA began show up as a problem. (Again, at this time, the book had not been written. And even when I did discover the book, it was a bit too late to reorient my failing marriage around some philosophical/psychological information.)

Here's how things began to play out as our upper-middle-class lifestyle became harder than it should've been.

Me: As a touch-oriented person, I sought out comfort through touch (cuddle, hold hands, kiss, spoon, nap, and yes, make love). I knew that I gained strength and calming closeness from physical touch in all its wonderful forms. So this is how I wanted to be comforted and this is how I chose to reach out to my then-wife.

Her: Her love language was more in the realm of "do something for me that shows me how you care." She wanted me to anticipate chores and just do them without having to be asked. She wanted the lawn to be mowed at a certain time without ever needing to tell me, or more likely, get in an argument with me about why it needed to happen this very weekend. She wanted action and not touch or comforting words.

As we began to hit tougher times, she began to focus on the "actions" I was or was not taking in support of her needs and feelings of stress and trauma. While I wanted to cuddle, she wanted to do the Excel spreadsheet for the afternoon to see where we'd spent all the money and where we were going to spend the money next week.

The trying times brought out our core love language orientation in a pronounced way. She became unable, or increasingly less willing, to bridge the gap to my touch requests, as she was so focused on the DO aspect of our relationship. I was so lost by the isolation of not being touched that I began to thrash a little bit, wondering if I were ever going to get a physical need met again.

Things did not work out. We were no longer willing to compromise our core needs, as articulated through our love language. We lost the connection that had bound us in the beginning, as we reoriented our wants and dreams around ourselves. Once we had unlocked the parenting portion of our needs (having kids) and had begun to experience some of the stresses of adult life as parents (bills, insurance, jobs, job loss, stay-at-home dreams), we began to act out our love language requirements in a more pronounced way.

It's a simple explanation for a complex situation, but it holds some clear truths. We started out our relationship and eventual marriage with abundant sexual energy and the thrill of newness and youth. We hit the mid-marriage period and, as stress developed, we experienced our losses and needs more directly in identifiable alliance to our love language profile. As we got clearer and more articulate about what we needed, neither of us was willing to give up any part of our needs to fulfill the needs of the other person. In the end, she decided to seek her satisfaction outside of the relationship to me, and we divorced. The differences in our love language DNA seem to hold the clearest description of what broke down.

As I move forward into my life, looking for another relationship, I am more acutely aware of several things.

- How happy is the person?
- Do they share the same love language of touch?

- How affectionate are they?
- Are they willing to own their own issues and take responsibility for their own happiness?
- Are they attractive to me?

From the joy comes an additive feature that I am looking to attract into my life. I am a meta-happy person. I can see the good in awful times and will work towards and keep striving towards solutions, knowing that my joyful optimism will prevail. But that is not always the case. So I hope to find another person who is also additive with her energy and happiness. AND who shares the love language of touch.

Wrapping all that up with in the form of a woman who is attractive to me and who finds me attractive… that will be the next unlocking of touch for me. And without that meta-quality set, I'm happy being alone with my dogs and cats while continuing to seek the touch of another toucher.

36.
Nothing Is as Exciting as New Love, Right?

The first step to recovery is admitting there's a problem.

Preamble: When the animal intoxication of chemical romance hits, our brains go on stun. We are no longer thinking like a human, we're more like a dog.

I'm not a greener pastures guy. I loved my wife. I loved my last girlfriend. Those relationships are over, in the romantic sense, so I prop my hopes backup and set off again on the epic quest. The chivalrous knight's journey. ARGGGH. I'm a bit exhausted from all the questing and leaping off after any romantic potential. I'm most tired of my optimistic fool's trait that keeps my heart engaged long after the true colors have been shown.

All we have is hope. When things go wrong, when disappointments happen, when "bad things happen to good people," all we have is our ability to imagine a better place, a new hope, a delayed gratification dream. Thank goodness for that, but good grief for all the times we have to fail to find another human to grow and evolve with. We keep trying.

Today I will try again. I will hope that "love" with the little "l" is out there and perhaps nearby. The last quest led to a brilliant woman, who dialed in my number physically and sexually, for some unknown reason. We don't really understand chemistry. We try to rationalize the "opposites attract" theme, but it doesn't make rational sense when we look at our preferences. I use a dog metaphor sometimes to illustrate, even to myself, the simple mystery of physical attraction.

> **Two dogs meet in a dog park. One of three things happens:**
> **1. One tail is wagging.**
> **2. Two tails are wagging.**
> **3. No tails are wagging.**

I think it has a lot less to do with our conscious brains and a lot more to do with something subconscious, sublingual, and more dog-like. I might think I have a thing for poodles and pitbulls. But when a fancy, just-my-type boxer enters the park, all my previous ideas of who/why/what I wanted are thrown to the wind. A whimsy of hormones, eye signals, body language, and something else... Magic. That's the only explanation for it. When magic happens, we are up for the pursuit. Our animal instincts kick in, and even across a room, we can spot the potential and feel the tiniest rush. If we are open to the signals, we might close in on the deal, attempt a proud display, and engage in courtship.

When both tails are wagging, there is a potential for magic. There is also potential for overlooking some egregious problems, some unfinished issues that are as plain as day to anyone standing nearby, but we've fallen into some other state. An altered state, and not always for the better. When the hit of sexual chemistry arrives, we are also vulnerable to euphoria, rushing into things, and premature sexual engagement. Fine. If you feel it, go for it. If you have insatiable lust and passion, go, do the animal thing, rut, pounce, devour. It's wonderful. But be aware, it's like an intoxication. And while you're intoxicated, you should not operate heavy machinery or get pregnant. (A joke and subtle safe-sex hint.)

So, let's say for illustration, you've got the chemistry with someone, and the rushing blood in your head and heart is an indication that you are getting intoxicated. Notice. Appreciate. And take a long drink of it. BUT… PLEASE… PAUSE…

Sorry. The headlong rush into sex and animal passions is awesome and fun and … Dangerous. I know I sound dramatic. But I am being dramatic on purpose. Let's see how I can make this clearer, less metaphorical. I'll get more personal and tell a little bit about my experience with the drug of love.

I have gone headlong into the night of intoxicated coupling. With two exceptions (in college, sort of one-night-stand variations), all of these rushed relationships have ended in fiery disasters. Hear me. Nothing is as exciting as new love. YES. I agree. And nothing is as blinding as the animal chemistry that kicks in somewhere below our human intelligence, and that blindness lasts for weeks, months, years if we're… that "lucky" or perhaps "tragically deceived."

Let me try again from the beginning. My first marriage was initiated by such flames and synchronicity that I spent the first 45 days of our "relationship" either in her bed or mine. Of course, we were just finishing college, we had time, we had the uncertainty of "what's next" in our lives. We had time and chemistry to burn. I knew on my honeymoon, however, when the fieriness showed up aimed at me rather than with me, that I had made a huge mistake marrying this woman. STRIKE ONE for hot sex.

My second marriage was a bit more stable, but the chemistry was no less mind-altering. I was still wounded from the flame-out of my first marriage and the wreckage that was left behind after she did her business of "divorcing me." So I fell effortlessly into romantic reverie when I ran into an old high school friend. And she was/is still beautiful to me. We attempted to be smart, we attempted to be honest and go slowly. The stars were already in place, and we were negotiating with seriously impaired intellect. Such is the role of the intoxication. We partner and mate for the good of the species.

So my second RUSH went that way. We spawned two beautiful children. Still, I should have never consummated this relationship. Red flags and issues within the first weeks should've could've would've made a more sober man say, "No thank you." I was sober of any artificial intoxicants, but I was as addicted to her beauty and body as any garden variety addict. I saw the danger. I responded to the warnings. I proceeded onward and inward. We married. Altered everything about our lives. Had kids. And things went off the rails, in part due to the disconnects I was getting warning signals about in those first few love-addled weeks, even before we'd ever slept together. I was too far gone to pull up from the terminal velocity nose dive. I gave it all. I put it all in. We both did.

The third RUSH ended last night. It should've ended months ago, when she calmly and forcefully broke up with me. But I was on the trail of exciting love. I was in the quest mode. I had gotten a taste of hot sex, and I was no more sober than a male tomcat around a female in heat. And I'm not making any judgments about her or the warning flares she was firing straight at me. I was well aware of the danger as I moved in for the conquest. I was as hungry as I've ever been and still wounded. But more lonely and ready and energetic.

When the females (and males) of many animal species show unhealthy signs, they are either ostracized and left behind or driven from the herd. I even had a friend telling me, "She's in no shape for a relationship." I had all the information I needed. Heck, when the woman is saying, "No, nope, nada, don't do it," while still welcoming you into her arms... well, that's your problem right there.

New love is a drug that might be more powerful than heroin. If we're addicted and activated, we're at risk of slipping back into unhealthy patterns of addiction, intoxication, regret, withdrawal, and repeat. Not a fun or survivable path. Addiction eventually kills us, if we don't get help.

I'm on my own for this one. I walked in "eyes wide shut" as they say. Knowing, seeing, being told, "This one is not for you," and going for it anyway. And five or six breakups later, it's hard to count them now, I'm finally sober enough to admit my problem.

The first step to recovery is admitting there's a problem.

Yep (hand raised). I have a problem with love.

37.

What Men Think About Sex Versus What a Woman Thinks They Think About

This is a response to Samantha Rodman's post, "What Men Think About Sex vs. Reality" (*Huffington Post*) – from a woman's perspective, albeit an educated sex therapist with a Ph.D. Still she's a woman. I'm a man. And I beg to differ, just a bit. (And I love Samantha Rodman, Ph.D., btw.)

Okay so let's crush a few of the stereotypes. Or, are we talking about college boys here? Let's quickly scan the list and see what pops out for debate.

> 1. Frequent and strong sexual desire and thoughts should be natural and normal for all people in long-term relationships. (**Boy:** Yep. / **Man:** Not by a long shot.)
>
> 2. Most married couples are having sex at least three times a week, if not more. (**Boy**, never been married: YES. / **Man**, married twice, divorced twice: Um, yeah, next myth.)
>
> 3. Women go into sex expecting and wanting the focus to be on their pleasure. (**Boy:** That's where the focus should be, right? / **Man:** Hyper-focus on anyone is a turn off, let's have a little play with our sex, shall we?)

4. Men who focus on a woman's pleasure (read: enjoy giving oral sex) are few and far between, but I myself happen to be one of these rare ones (Dr. Rodman noted 80% to 100% of her male clients think this). (**Boy:** I'm eager to learn, eager to please: Yes. / **Man:** I do love it, but it's only part of the fun: a qualified YES.)

5. I must last as long as I can and be in full control of myself at all times. (**Boy:** Because anything less is premature ejaculation. / **Man:** Losing control is part of the fun and turn-on for men and women: NO.)

6. Also, I should engage in a lot of foreplay, all the time, because women want this. (**Boy:** Women have longer warmup cycles: YES. / **Man:** Sometimes, but sometimes a quickie is what's in order.)

7. Women orgasm from intercourse alone pretty frequently. (**Boy:** Even I've heard this is false, hence all the focus on oral sex: Not really. / **Man:** Old ideas die hard: NO.)

8. The women I dated in high school/college/my 20s whom I had lots of crazy sex with are still doing that with the men they married. (**Boy:** And all women love to have sex, right: Sure. / **Man:** But we're not in our 20s, and sex takes planning and effort, if you're even able to talk them into it: No.)

9. My wife makes up excuses not to have sex, and other women just go with the flow and are happy to feel desired. (**Boy:** Everyone is having more sex than me: YES. / **Man:** Well, there does seem to be some connection between clean dishes and sexual desire,

but there's a lot more to the equation: NO.)

10. After the baby, most women get their sex drive back reasonably quickly. (**Boy:** I'm guessing at this, because I've never been with a woman who's had a baby: Okay. / **Man:** Um, I don't have any data to determine "reasonably quickly" so I'm going to ask the experts on Google: No.)

11. Watching porn does nothing to hurt our sex life or relationship. (**Boy:** It makes me a better lover: Agreed. / **Man:** It depends on the relationship: Porn is not the problem, the relationship might be. NO. Porn in general is not harmful to healthy relationships, as long as there's no porn addiction.)

So those are my answers. And while I'm no sex expert or marriage counselor, I have enough sense to know that this list was generated from clinical observations. At least the people in question were working on their relationship. So they are a long way from the possible "norm" cave man mentality. But somehow, a few of these "truths" feel like "myths" that need to be busted. Or that have been busted and passed on a long time ago, but maybe are still tossed around in clinical settings for what's going on.

Porn

Let's start with **porn**. Porn is like a drug or alcohol. Some people can use it and not abuse it or suffer the fallout of addiction and withdrawal. To say that porn is harmful to marriages is simply not true. It's like an old wives' tale that women have been using to hammer us men for quite some time. And what about the couples who like to watch porn together? Or porn that is used when the wife is disabled or unable/unwilling to be intimate? Is that killing the marriage, or is that a way for the man to still have some sexual fun without leaving the marriage? Porn is not the issue. The relationship and perhaps the couple's relationship to porn or their own sexuality could be a problem. It's up for discussion, but it cannot be written off as evil or corrupting. It's simply porn. Some do and some don't.

Frequent and passionate sex throughout our lifetimes as a married couple

Um, yeah, on what planet? Planet Libido? Sex and sexual desire take work on both partners' roles. And both men and women can experience highs and lows of sexual desire. In a long-term relationship a lot of factors begin to come into play. Stress and exhaustion are the two top killers or sexual desire. And add a little depression in either partner to that mix and you quickly see that sex is a negotiation and dance. It's not a given. The recent studies showing how women in monogamous relationships tend to lose sexual desire are like old news. We've been talking about the seven-year itch forever. Did you assume it was just about men? Both partners have to work at staying sexual interested in their partners. Sure, a new partner might seem to offer renewed vigor, and perhaps that's one of the reasons divorce rates have skyrocketed, but to keep in tune and sexually interested in your life-partner is an ever-changing quest. I was all for it and would've worked at it continuously. My ex-wife and mother of my kids had other ideas.

Oral sex, vaginal orgasms, foreplay

Good lord women, we're all in this together. This information is fairly new, but if we're even half interested in pleasing a woman, we're reading about it on the cover of *Cosmo* in the checkout line. These types of hints and tips are everywhere, not telegraphed, frickin' broadcast to all of us, men and women. Fact is, a lot of men and women don't like oral sex. In a divorce recovery class when the topic was brought up (25 men and 25 women), the split was about 25% didn't enjoy it, 25% really loved it, 50% were okay either way. And for all the times we're told to go slow, get into the foreplay, to somehow have this thrown back at us as something we're doing wrong. What? Okay, the big issue here is communication. That's hard. Talking about sex, asking for what you want DURING sex, that's hard.

Why aren't we having sex again?

This is a loaded topic. And yes, in general, the woman is the excuse maker. But that's part of nature's little game. You see it in peacocks every day. Do you think the male peacock is getting frustrated at showing his handsome feathers? No, it's just what he does. He says, "I'm ready. I'm willing. I'm gorgeous. What about you?" And in the human species we have some of the same rituals.

My ready and willing proposal: "I'm honest. I'm fitter than I was a year ago. I'm feeling sexy. How about after we do the dishes together I draw you a nice bath and put the kids to bed." The woman can say, "No thanks." Or, perhaps leave an opening, "I'm not feeling it right now, but the bath does sound nice. Let's finish the dishes, and start there…"

There's no right or wrong way to ask about sex. There are plenty of ways to turn off the options immediately. The issue is more about communication. It's fine if the male is more driven by his t-score. And women are more attracted by romance, a clean house, and all the bills being paid. It's just slightly different wiring. But it's not all that different from the caveman who ran out and risked his life for the tribe while hunting down dinner. And the cavewoman prepared the fire, dried the fur bedding, and was ready to cook when the meat was brought home. If there was energy left in the warrior after all that, and the woman was still awake, a little rutting could be a welcome thing. But I have a hard time imagining a caveman being all self-conscious when his woman fell asleep directly after dinner.

Sex is a complex dance. We've got to have better communication about it. I'm no fine example. It can be difficult just to say, "Um, can you try this?" But it's part of the education we must go through to learn the ways and means of our partner. And life-partners get to know us better than anyone. So we can find all sorts of ways, over time, to turn them on and turn them upside down crazy. IF we're looking for them, and asking about them, and continuing to work on our parts.

Perhaps too much of our sex lives has become routine and lazy. And the stereotypical male who gets his and rolls off to go to sleep still exists. I'm sure he's out there. But his days are numbered. As women wake up to their needs and their own power, they're asking for more. Oral, maybe. Frequency, as determined by prior arrangement. Foreplay or animal sex, depending on situation and available time.

Sex is fun to think about. It's more fun to explore. But we often don't get enough time to explore the nuance of making love to the same beautiful person year after year. And if men or women get bored with their partner, or think the 20-somethings in porn are more to our taste, the responsibility is on them to either wake up and get to work or leave for greener pastures. It's kind of harsh, but that's the reality these days.

What Men Think About Sex Versus What a Woman Thinks They Think About

Enough with the myths and truths. Let's find out what our partner thinks and wants. Let's ask them. Let's return the favor and tell them our dirty little fantasies, too.

VI

Sleeping Over

As your relationship deepens, you need to make your priorities and desires clear. The single dad has ideas of his own. How do you get the conversation started about, "What are we doing? What about us?" Don't smother him just because you're sleeping with him. Help everyone keep their perspective and priorities straight during the early phases of relationship building.

38.

Is it Love We're After?

There are three types of love, as I described in the Three Loves chapter.

Eros is often thought of as the love of sex. But it's much more than sexual. It's the fire, the passion, the drive to create. Much of my eros, or erotic energy, has been focused on finding a partner and funneled away from the other creative passions.

Filial love is family, community, connectedness. This is the love you are washed in, sitting alone with friends.

Agape love is the flat-out powerful love of the creator, however you care to imagine her. All part of the whole. However you chose to believe, however you chose to be amazed, that is the god of Agape. And while it can be sustaining, it is not nourishing in the same way as the first two. And certainly not as filling and energetic as the first one, Eros.

Walking around the lake with my "special friend," we were discussing our relationship. She was being funny for a bit, teasing me about what our relationship was and was not. "Well, we're not dating," I said. "Because I don't want to date."

"Okay, well what are we then?"

"I don't know. I don't have any name for it," I said, attempting to be honest and exploring the idea of what we had become. "So," I said, "You don't want a long-term relationship, and I don't want to date. We're even. I don't even care what you call it, whatever we're in." We agreed that we didn't have the name or definition of what we were becoming, or even what we were at that moment, in a tender morning of "just being together" and grooving on that. And we walked on and talked about many things.

And somewhere along the way, the word "love" was mentioned. And it's become a more casual and easy word, not huge, or dramatic. Like LOVE. And I appreciated her sincerity. And I have been trying to understand just what she meant by it for a week or so, since the word came up. We've been talking about love in many ways. As in, you love someone deeply and will always remain friends, no matter what. We have that. And then there's all that other stuff...

So what love are we, as newly divorced adults, after? Are we wanting love, Love, or LOVE. I think there are escalating forms of this word love. Some of them have to do with desire and passion. Other parts, the bigger parts, have to do with "what's next" or "what we will become." Today I am sure we have "love," the first stage along the path. And that's enough. And I would guess, right along schedule (though I have no real knowledge of what I'm talking about) for a well-matched relationship. Too soon and you risk mixing up lust and love. Too easily and you're talking more about lust or capture. We don't want capture at this point.

Love is a growing of intention between two people. As we walk, around the trail and on with our lives, we get a chance to be with the other person. And if we are comfortable about going slowly, we can see more sides of this other person, while we are still building our trust and caring for him or her. In my marriage, I was drawn in much too quickly to love and Love. We were dating and then living together in a matter of six months. We, of course, were on a mission to become parents, and in our late 30s, so we moved through our own internal objections and sped up the process. But we missed a few warning signs along the way that might have prevented us from getting married had we been less enamored.

So if love comes too quickly, you might be tempted to overlook some of the issues in the early months of the relationship. By keeping things in the lower-case love, you can ferret things out better. Neither of us is interested in moving in together. Neither of us is interested in becoming step-parents. And we are both working to keep our own trajectories intact while beginning to bend some of the time towards being with the other person. I think it's best to remain in this early-stage love until some true burning desire comes up between the two of you to move things to the next stage. Again, I am not there, at the moment. I am very comfortable with hearing "love" in my friend's statements. And I am happy to reflect the sentiment. But I understand that we may not be on the same page about what love is or what we are talking about.

The two of us have been through a lot already. We've jumped through some burning hoops to see the next layer of protection being stripped away. We are pretty close to the pure joy of finding time together and knowing that we will enjoy the company of this other person until something else comes along.

And here's where our current discussions tend to veer in slightly different directions. She has said, in the past, that she's not into a long-term relationship. And I have accepted this frame in our courtship. Today, when I mentioned this to her, she winced. She wanted to explain, or to refer me back to her emails. But I was clear in my mind. I do want a long-term relationship. I am into this for the long haul. And if we continue to grow as partners, I am eventually going to want to grow into Love, the capital "L" version, that asks, what's next? But that's a ways down the path. And putting too much emphasis or worry about this eventual crossroads is premature.

Today we are together. I don't have a name for what we are. I am not "dating" her, because I have decided with my heart that I am in relationship with her and we are not just casually getting together.

In practice, however, we are casually getting together. And we are getting together when our schedules allow. That she's not into a long-term relationship is also a frame that is being contested. What I think she means is she has no way to think about or imagine what the capital-L Love would look like. I don't either, but I don't need to go there to know that's where I'm going. Eventually.

She once asked me, "Well, if you like relationships so much, why have you only had three in the four years since you've been divorced?"

"Because," I said, smiling inwardly, "It is more important for me to spend time building a real relationship than it is for me to date a lot of women." So there (here) we are.

39.

I Sing the Body Connected: Cultivating Sexual Energy

> Within there runs blood,
> The same old blood! the same red-running blood!
> There swells and jets a heart, there all passions, desires, reachings, aspirations...
> – *I Sing the Body Electric, Walt Whitman*

I was walking around the lake with a male friend, and we were comparing notes on sex and the energy it produces. Just the idea of sex, the opportunity of sex, is enough to quicken the heartbeat, inspire the discipline of exercise and eating right. And once the connection has been established, even with a woman who may not be a perfect match, an energy, a confidence, a glow transforms every cell of our bodies.

Are women like this? I don't know. But I can tell you, when I have been having regular sex, I am a different person. I walk in the world with a different confidence and a different smile. I have a joy that radiates from within and is infinitely more attractive, as the sexually active and attractive male, to the women around me. So sex begets more sex. Or so the idea goes.

I recall the wonderful warmth I would get in my marriage, when we made arrangements to have sex. It could be as simple as asking for a time after I delivered the kids to school for us to "be together." It was a magical agreement. And once in place I would energetically pack the kids, make breakfast, and get them off to school. My then-wife could lounge around in bed or take a bath, if that's what she wanted to do... I was IN and on my way to "having sex." Woohoo.

That thrill never ceased in my marriage. And even as my offers were turned down at an alarming rate, I was still "into her." I was still propositioning her and waiting for the moment, the chemistry, the chores and bills to be paid, whatever... I was still desirous of my wife. She, however, was heading in some other direction. I can't illuminate the cause of the her ever-lowering libido, but I'm sure the stresses of life, mid-life, and figuring out what to do with her career were all weighing on her heavily.

We moved on and, after some varying efforts, divorced. And the world of sex opened up again like some fantasy. Unfortunately, the reality of dating after divorce was more fantasy than reality, but the prospects of new sex, new women, new opportunities were enough to keep my optimism high even while my success rate was low. And I was really the main problem. I wasn't really ready for a relationship or sex. I had no idea what casual sex meant, and I was wounded deeply by the crash landing of the divorce.

It took a long time and a lot of effort to get myself back into fighting shape, or courting shape, as it might be. And only recently have I unlocked any of the previous rules that might inhibit me from going for a tryst with a woman I don't find 100% alluring. I am still most interested in a primary relationship that becomes exclusive the minute the bedroom is brought into the equation. But I am also interested in understanding what my drive towards permanent relationships is, when both of mine have ended in failure. Am I willing to suspend monogamy for something else?

Clearly I am still figuring it out. Life and dating post-divorce is an amazing process. In several of the features of this life progression I am less than 100% successful. But my hopefulness keeps popping me back up to the surface, even after disasters and divorce terrors have pulled me or my financial life underwater. I keep surfacing. I keep heading back to shore and preparing to start again.

At what?

That's the real question. I know the power of sex and relationships on me and my self-esteem. And I know that the collapse of this marriage was one of the most trying moments of my life. And those trying moments keep rearing their heads over and over at the most inopportune time. It's hard.

But what is my hurry? Am I really looking for Ms. Lovejoy? Am I more interested in playing the field than I might have been in my 20s or 30s?

I am certainly more interested in understanding the attraction I have to women of all shapes and forms. It's more the joy I'm after, when trying to find a fit with a woman. I have found several near misses, but the fit was off. It's the happiness that comes from them that attracts me back towards them.

In my life I have learned to deal with significant disappointments and still open up the next day with a "let's go" attitude. My joy is not connected directly to the everyday ups and downs of life, work, love, divorce, parenting, health, and… relationships. I'd rather be alone than in a relationship with a destructive woman. I'd rather masturbate than wind up with someone who throws passive aggressive barbs with every other text. And of course, it's not just about the sex.

But sex between two willing adults has a powerful effect on

me. And while I am not dependent on that energy, it does provide some amazing opportunities for creative expression and growth.

There's a down side to the sexual playground as well. Some people are not ready to have any kind of romantic relationship. A lot of people, actually. You can hear it when they talk about their ex or their struggles with parenting. You can tell in the way they don't touch back, or they don't express spontaneous affection. Stress is a powerful turn-off. Why would anyone willingly get into a relationship with a stressed-out partner? No matter how amazing they are physically, if their mental state is depressed or fragile, it's going to be a no-win relationship in my experience.

So I'm looking for joy. I'm asking for a happy response from the women I see. I'm listening when they talk about their lives and their ex and their kids, chores, work, love, and ambitions. And if they don't have ambitions, if they can't tell me what they are passionate about, well, that's an issue for me.

I want you to be happy. I want to feel the electrical current connect between us when we are together. I'd love to feel the flush of desire when we make arrangements to take off our clothes together.

But as the current is interrupted, I can walk away from bad connections. A connection might be more like a hookup, but that's not what I'm looking for. That's why the new dating apps, Tinder and others, are not very interesting to me. They might offer a lot of potential electrical hookups, but they are not sustainable. Someone looking for that kind of relationship is going to stay in that kind of relationship in the long run.

In the long run I hope to find another woman who turns me on in the same way my wife did, even after 11 years of marriage. I'm not asking for her again, but someone I can pour my current into. And this time, someone who can continue to feed some of the energy, enthusiasm, and joy back to me for recycling.

I Sing the Body Connected: Cultivating Sexual Energy

> I sing the body connected, with the same red blood that awakes in the morning with a start, with the same red blood that cuddles and curls at night and still longs for you...
> – *i sing the body connected*, John McElhenney

40.

Sexual Desire: Men & Women, the Chemistry Between Us

According to science, testosterone is what regulates sexual desire. And, as expected, men have a lot more of it than women, both the hormone and the desire for sexual activity. That's a fact of our biological evolution. Men hunt for food and available mating partners. It's in our DNA. But in the modern world, can these sexual differences cause problems or be the key to opening up a better balance in our sexual compatibility?

One place to look for the variation between men and women is Indiana University's 2009 National Survey of Sexual Health and Behavior, conducted with 5,865 Americans ages 14 to 94. FiveThirtyEight's Mona Chalabi analyzed the masturbation data to create the infographic below.

How Often Do You Masturbate?
Responses by age and sex, 2009

WOMEN	18-24	25-29	30-39	40-49	50-59	60-69	70+
Not in past year	36.5%	28.5%	37.0%	35.3%	46.2%	54.0%	68.6%
A few times per year to monthly	28.6	37.2	30.5	38.3	36.7	35.7	26.1
A few times per month to weekly	24.5	21.5	22.0	19.8	13.9	9.8	4.8
2-3 times per week	7.3	7.9	9.0	5.2	2.6	0.3	0.0
>4 times per week	3.1	5.0	1.5	1.5	0.7	0.3	0.5

MEN	18-24	25-29	30-39	40-49	50-59	60-69	70+
Not in past year	18.5%	16.5%	20.1%	24.0%	28.1%	38.8%	53.6%
A few times per year to monthly	16.9	14.7	18.8	19.8	24.3	29.3	23.5
A few times per month to weekly	25.0	25.4	27.0	25.0	23.7	18.0	14.0
2-3 times per week	20.8	23.4	20.6	16.8	17.5	10.1	7.3
>4 times per week	18.8	20.1	13.5	14.4	6.4	3.8	1.7

FIVETHIRTYEIGHT   SOURCE: NATIONAL SURVEY OF SEXUAL HEALTH AND BEHAVIOR

Infographic credited to Mona Chalabi and FiveThirtyEight.

If we take self-pleasure as an indication of sexual desire, we can see some stark contrasts between men and women. About 1/3 of the women between the ages of 18 and 50 listed their masturbation frequency as "not in the past year." After 50 that percentage jumps to 50% and on up to 70% for our elder ladies. Now men show the same tapering off with age, but look at the men listing masturbation over four times per week (PER

WEEK!): 15-19% of men between the ages of 18 and 50 reported masturbating over four times per week. Wow.

No wonder my masturbation-related posts seem so natural to me and are kind of icky to some of my women friends. Fascinating. Perhaps masturbation is not the perfect indicator of sexual desire, but the contrast between men and women is fairly dramatic, don't you think?

So we men are walking around with testosterone raging around in our veins and brains at a high level into our 50s. We are constantly driven towards release. And it must be fatiguing for the women in our lives to have to deal with that much aggressive sexual pressure. Thank goodness men (and even monkeys) have learned to release the raging hormones via masturbation.

So what do you do with a relationship between men and women when the request for sex is constant and unrelenting? Well, of course, the man needs to figure out a way to pleasure himself, or he's going to be frustrated a lot of the time. And it's really not the woman's responsibility, even in a marriage, to pleasure us. It's a dance. We men are constantly asking for, thinking about, and craving sex. Women, not so much.

I read recently about how women need a bit more ramp-up time to get in the mood. Sexual desire is not something that drives their daily motivations. The suggestion from a woman for women was, instead of saying no all the time, to say, "Let's see how you might be able to get me in the mood."

In my experience the imbalance is manageable as long as the relationship is in good shape. If the conversation and trust are still intact in the marriage, the constant pressure from the man can become more of a game, rather than an irritation. When things were working for us, sex was just a part of our play. Sure, I was in heat more of the time, and she was able to pleasure me efficiently and quickly in the shower as we were getting ready for work. And it was easy, often involving contact and rubbing rather than penetration.

But when the relationship begins to go south, the sexual communication becomes more and more strained. And sure, women cannot satisfy our every craving. That's not their responsibility. But the dynamic is there either way. If you're not talking about it, or playing about it, it's getting built up, and the imbalance may become more and more painful.

That was the big indicator to me that things were not working at all in my marriage. I was fine with self-pleasure for long periods of time, but ZERO sexual connection over a month began to get my attention. And ultimately this is the pain that I woke up to and began expressing in my marriage as complaint and dissatisfaction. Again, I'm not talking about daily or even weekly sex. I'm talking about going a month without so much as an encouraging touch. Nothing. Nada. Zilch. Something was out of whack, and my whacking was not going to repair it.

Sex is an important part of any relationship. For those of us who are more touch oriented, a lack of sexual connection is akin to starvation. In the last year of my marriage I was not just sex starved, I was touch starved. There was so little affection coming from her that when she said, "I love you" one night, out of the blue, I felt an immense pain. I realized for the first time how infrequent her expressions of affection of any kind had become.

That was the beginning of my campaign to have her either return to the marriage or divorce me. It wasn't my idea. But I was aware that the lack of touch was killing me. There was no amount of masturbation that was going to make up for the distance between us.

41.

Beyond the Rush of Love Is the Test of Time

We seek a connection, a rush, a hit of passion. We search for our next relationship, sometimes in a wounded state, sometimes strong and confident. The process is the same. In starts and fits we meet people, we check out the chemistry, the attraction, and then we evaluate their potential as a partner. As we spend time together, we lean into the connections we find, the affinities we try to cultivate and highlight. And the red flags we try to evaluate and either dispel or bring up for discussion. A few too many red flags and we are out.

If we're lucky, we continue down the courting road towards whatever is next. Depending on our desire and openness, we progress on to the big-R Relationship. And sometimes we find ourselves afraid to explore that road for long without fear kicking in. What's that fear about?

Part of the fear, for me, is the knowledge that my desire and romantic goggles will cloud my clear thinking and I will be blind-sided by some fatal flaw in the relationship or the other person, or even our fractured match. A flip side to that fear is the one that says, Oh my, what if it continues to grow and build and feel great? What if it's mutual? And that too has a fear base: going too far and too fast into a relationship that ultimately has the power to destroy your hard-won recovery.

So we balance our feelings between the two extremes, walking together down the old road of becoming familiar with each other's habits, quirks, and even fears. If we've done our self-care homework and are coming from a healthy and stable place within ourselves, we can parse the various emotions that come flooding up from the highs and lows of this journey.

It can't all be euphoria and bright stars. If there is zero conflict and only bliss, something is amiss. You can be assured that the opium of your bliss will give way to the hangover at some point, and the real "other" person will show up. It's hard to remember that the courting phase also puts each of us on our best behavior, whereas when we become increasingly close, we start to let a few of our skeletons out. On accident, for example, if we snore or something. And unconsciously we may project past hurts and memories onto this new relationship. Either way, if you have zero conflict, you'd better dig into that, because a healthy fight or healthy disagreement is essential to success for the long haul. You've got to be able to disagree and not freak out when you find things that don't gel.

Okay, so let's say all of this is working. And let's imagine you're several months down the treacherous road, you've weathered an argument or two, maybe even seen and worked through a few red flags. And it's still feeling good. What then?

Then comes the biggest fear, in my opinion. What if you do everything right and explore all skeletons and mismatches, and something still starts to go off. Maybe in a year, maybe in five years. How do you keep a relationship healthy? How do you still develop passion for a person you've been exploring with for years? What's the key to sustained and loving relationships?

Because, after all this work to get where you are, to even come close to finding a compatible partner, the worst thing imaginable is the death of that passion or compassion for the other person. How did it happen in your previous relationships? What was the fracture that started the breakdown in the relationship? Was it a specific event?

In my experience so far, part of the hesitation and "go slow" impulses comes from a healthy respect for this potential let down. I don't want to get deep with someone if I'm likely to get hurt. And in the early months of the relationship, I can assure you the novelty and newness, the excitement for discovery, fuel a distorted view of reality. It's okay to go slow. The main goal is communication and understanding how you and your partner cope under pressure. It can't all be paradise and nectar.

In my real marriage (my first marriage was a trial run), I was still madly in love with my partner when she began to look elsewhere for that connection. There was no physical infidelity but a few big slips of the emotional variety. Through it all, we both struggled to recapture, reframe, and reform our relationship. And ultimately, even as I was optimistic and willing for repair, the other person decided divorce would be the better course of action for us.

That was the real death of my relationship, learning that my then-wife had been to see an attorney to see what divorce looked like, to explore options.

I hope never to experience that free-fall drop again in my life. I'd rather stay alone, or at least casual and superficial. The breakdown of my marriage and thus family was the hardest moment I have yet to experience. As I rebuild my life, and rebuild my trust for another person, the fall is one of those skeletons that I have to keep expressing and being honest about. And if we stay in the present moment, and keep our connection, we're on the way towards building a bridge over past hurts and fears and towards what each of us is ultimately looking for: a life-long cheerleader and partner. Someone who can see the hurts and quirks and still love you through them.

It's a long road just to find a person who's willing to even venture down the relationship journey at all. So how do we build a new connection without allowing the fear or euphoria to blind us to the real relationship? Again, it's about staying in the present moment. You don't have to plan or fear commitment when you are just getting to know someone. You don't have to protect yourself if you stay in the "now" and just enjoy the process and the high of a new relationship.

Look for ways to see through the haze of lust, or the fog of fear, to recognize when things are working or things are really not working. It takes time. There is no hurry.

VII

New Horizons

Is it time to discuss marriage again? Do you want to get married? What are the advantages of not becoming man and wife? Once you do decide to rejoin, what are the steps to make sure everyone in the family, in both families, is on board? Pitfalls and solutions to the marriage question. If you're ready to make the commitment, let your heart and your love guide you, and the kids and the relationship will follow your lead.

42.

Whole Adult Beings: Knowing Ourselves, Knowing What We Won't Compromise

One night I had the pleasure of eating dinner with an old friend from out of town and his new girlfriend. When he texted me that he was in town he said, "Down here with new girlfriend. Recently divorced but all good." I was surprised but not all that surprised. Seems like this divorce thing is going around. And my friends and I are in the 7- to 11-year-itch period where the rubber meets the road. So he was divorced and already traveling with his "new girlfriend." Wow. Good for him.

It was great to see my friend and his delightful new partner. She too is the survivor of divorce, with two kids who are a bit younger than mine and my friend's. We had a very interesting discussion about what we were doing with our lives.

You see, in addition to catching up with my friend, whom I hadn't spent time with in over two years, we were also catching up as a group of recently divorced people. I took the opportunity to explore some ideas I'd been kicking around.

Here's what seems to ring true for all of us.

> 1. We start marriage with a set of assumptions and a set of ideals.
>
> 2. Over time, as we add mortgages, kids, and health insurance to the equation, we begin a long process of adaption and compromise.

3. If we continue to compromise away from our true selves, we will eventually get depressed or angry. We will start looking for a way back to something more vibrant, more authentic. We want to get back to sometime more like the ME I remember.

4. Divorce happens. Initialized by one of the party, and then the transformation begins.

5. In the process of divorce recovery we either (a) jump right back into another relationship, failing to examine or learn from what failed in the previous one, or (b) take some time to rediscover our solo-selves.

6. As somewhat activated solo-selves, we are now able to reclaim our artistic passions, our authentic aspirations, our alone-wants and our alone-desires.

7. In imagining and testing the concept of dating and relating to another adult human, we have new "non-negotiables" as part of our needs.

8. We do not want to re-enter the path of compromise and collapse of this newly rediscovered self.

9. We are forced to create something new.

As the three of us talked about our dreams for ourselves, we were careful to listen to the other person's dreams. I was sounding out and exploring my friend's musical aspirations. I wanted to hear about his new symphonic ideas. I was interested in the part of himself that he was rediscovering and re-establishing. And his new girlfriend was clearly in that same camp. She too was an artist. She had vision and drive. She wanted the musician in my friend to reignite and come alive.

So how can we enter into a new kind of relationship, now knowing what we know about ourselves? How will the mistakes of our past reframe what is and is not acceptable in our next relationship? And ultimately, can we create a Relationship 3.0 that keeps our goals and ambitions as creative individuals at the forefront of the mix WHILE we negotiate the togetherness that we also want?

I am curious how much of relationship is about sex for me. And if sex was more a function of several "dates," perhaps I would not need a relationship so much. I don't think that's it. I KNOW there is much more about relationships than sex. And I have decided that sex without the deeper connection is much more like masturbation. But it is interesting to pull apart all the aspects of relationship and see which parts of it are valuable and which parts are limiting.

At the moment I am limitless. I am alone, yes, but I am the sole determiner of what I am doing tonight. (Well, I have my kids this weekend, so not tonight...) And then I can ask what am I willing to give up to be WITH someone. What would "tonight" look like if another person were waiting in the wings to spend time with me?

Often in the early months of my courtship with the ex-y, we would have breakfast on a weekend and make plans to get back together in the early evening. And off we would go to our separate artist studios. (For the most part, art is a solo endeavor.) These were some of our happiest times.

When she let the work and compromise of our relationship kill her artistic dream, she became small and resentful of mine. I have never stopped trying to write songs or poems and stories. It takes time. And for sure, time away from the relationship.

So in defining and finding a next relationship, what time am I willing to be flexible on and what time am I going to keep just for myself?

43.

Love Is the Goal, Discover Your Own Path

"In love lies the seed of our growth. The more we love, the closer we are to the spiritual experience." – Paulo Coehlo

A simple quote and image on Facebook today triggered a thought I've been nurturing for quite some time. Love is the goal, yes, but LOVE as a state of being can happen at anytime and over some fairly trivial things. The point is to notice when LOVE enters your life and do more of what makes you feel those warm fuzzy feelings.

I love my breakfast. I crave it in the mornings. That's a good indication that my body is getting some benefit from the combination of yogurt and low-sugar granola. But the experience of longing and fulfillment that happens each morning is a teacher. I enjoy the craving. I enjoy the act of eating and savoring the meal. And I enjoy the warmth I get from being satisfied with my meal. It's a perfect relationship.

That's sort of how we want our relationships with people as well. Crave them when they are not with you. Enjoy and savor them when they are with you. And feel the complete fullness of life when you have been satiated by them. And I'm not just talking about sex here. Satiation comes from the ritual of the morning as you wake up together. Make sure you appreciate your partner just for being there. Celebrate what you have, getting ready, making coffee, eating breakfast. Celebrate the time you are together.

It's the longing that can get us in trouble. We long for our connection, and we turn to other things. I really like ice cream. But my craving for ice cream is different from my craving for my partner. They are also similar. I can sublimate my desire for love in many ways. I get that fuzzy feeling during and after eating ice cream, but I don't get any of the other warm fuzzies that true caring and nurturing can bring. Ice cream is a hollow craving. And ice cream bears no love for me.

My mate, on the other hand, lights up with my attention and affection. What I give in love I receive back in laughter and kisses. This is the space we'd love to live in. And then… there's all that other living we have to do. Parenting, if you have kids. Earning a living, to make the ship go. Exercise, so you have a long and healthy life. And chores, the struggle to stay one step ahead of entropy.

As we can remember our beloved during the day, we can remind ourselves of our deep love and craving of that other person. And this is not obsession, this is healthy desire. I don't want to control or manipulate her, I just want to be beside her, touching the small of her back, whispering my joys into her ear. And you can do this with little connective texts throughout the day, "You crossed my mind and stayed there." Little competitions between you, "How far have you walked today?" And little messages of caring, "I'm stopping by the store, is there anything you need or desire?"

Just letting the other person know you are thinking about them is a great first step in connecting for the long haul. Make sure you celebrate each other. Find the things you love to do together and do them. Make time for those things. Discover new things you might both like to do. And get out there and do them. An active love is much better than a sedentary love. If you love doing activities together, you get a double boost, love and endorphins. Go for it. Stay connected and celebratory as much as you can. There is plenty of time for the mundane, but it's tapping into the extraordinary that's the key to a long-lasting love affair.

44.

What's This About: Marriage?

Would you do it again? What's the point? Is it symbolism or security you seek? I don't know, but I'm willing to ask myself the questions about why I would ever want to get married again.

It came up in a recent discussion. "I don't think I'll ever do that again," she said.

I noticed my reaction. "Hmm. I wonder what that's about." But I quickly turned the observation inward to try and parse out what I would want from marriage. Let's see…

> 1. I already have kids, so it is not about them or their having a mom.
>
> 2. I did love the ring. I loved what it symbolized. I cried the first time I took it off. I was a proud husband.
>
> 3. Financially there are some advantages.
>
> 4. Security. (Hmm. This is the hardest one.)

In the end, the marriage did not provide any security within my relationship. I mean, perhaps she would have decided to seek greener pastures sooner had it not been for the legal and financial wranglings that were required to divorce me. But from my side, perhaps I was a bit blind-sided by my unrealistic trust in the "marriage" part of our relationship.

So what kind of trust could be won from getting married again? Would it make our bond any more secure?

The woman I was chatting with responded to my financial comment by asking, "Is that really something you considered when getting married?"

"No," I said, "But I would have to consider it a reason now. I mean we both have kids, so it wouldn't be about them."

And here we are, at the crux of the matter. Would MARRIAGE, the ring, the ceremony, the step-kid thing, give either of us more security? I don't know. Is it part of my plan? Perhaps, but it is certainly not something I think of in the early months of a relationship. Although she did catch me saying, "If a relationship doesn't have the potential of going long-term, then I'm not really interested."

"What does that even mean, long-term?" she asked, with a sly smile.

"I don't know."

45.

Learning to Love In the Present Moment

Love your time and be aware how you spend it.
Love your body and be aware how you use it.
Love your thoughts and be aware how you focus them.
Love your feelings and how they move you. *

How many ways to we project our stuff onto others? How many ways was the divorce, or end of the relationship, due to some illusion we held about the other person, or about our ability to change them. As harsh as it sounds, I believe that waiting or working to make the other partner change is a dead end. It never happens. It's like the family praying for the alcoholic to change and stop drinking. You need to get help for yourself, not the alcoholic.

So we travel on now, newly divorced and looking to find another chance to do it right. Or at least, do it better. Let's start with the reality versus the illusion. And I have to admit, I do this A LOT. I'm a romantic. Not a hopeless one, a hopeful one. Maybe that's the most dangerous kind.

As an adult I have many more creative ways to express myself than the last time I was "dating" or even before that, my college years, where I established some sort of idea how a date should go. Then I believed the old adage of giving them just a little bit of affection and then leaving them alone until they crave you, or you crave them, again. That idea of the heart growing fonder with absence. As an adult I don't actually buy into that concept.

But I sometimes go to the other extreme, and that's not any better.

As you might have guessed, I over-share all the time. I'm just so interested in sharing my ideas and reveries that I do it all the time. I can see that in an early phase of establishing boundaries and guidelines of a relationship with me, that I bleed all over the lines. I'm out of bounds all the time. And then I dial it back. And then I do it again.

A few things are at play here.

> 1. I'm enjoying the pursuit. I love the racing thoughts and romantic desires. I use the catalyst of sexual energy and desire as fuel to create. I let my heart fly and fantasize. I go with it.
>
> 2. I can get fooled by my own enthusiasms. I begin, even a tiny bit, to believe the over-inflated myth of passion I am responsible for creating.
>
> 3. From the receiver's point of view, I can come across as fixated and obsessed. And I wonder sometimes if they are right. Is love an obsession? Is romantic reverie a disease? It's certainly a distortion.
>
> 4. I occasionally have a hard time dialing back the streams of creativity. Often these are songs, poems, stories that are trying hard to capture this essence of love.
>
> 5. I don't love myself with the same passion I focus on other objects of desire.

One of my challenges in life, and certainly in relationship, is balancing the creative with the real. I occasionally have to strip back the romantic facade and realise I'm over-romanticizing.

This other person (ex-wife, lover, first date) can't possibly be all I am capable of projecting onto them. And that's one of my gifts too, diving deep into the romantic love vibe, extracting some form of uber-love. Some channeling of Eros.

But when I can't separate the myth from the person, I know I'm starting to go off the deep end. In recent dating experiences I have flushed a potential bird out of the nest with my charm only to scare the crap out of the bird with over-communication. I've never experienced the reverse, so I can't speak from experience. Then a date asked me what I might feel like if the poems and stuff were coming from her towards me.

I had to think about it. I guess I would be a bit overwhelmed. There, I learn again, I am overwhelming. I have a tendency to overwhelm others. Okay. I can watch that.

And really, I believe that I am in control, that I can stop at any time. But my heart and mind don't always obey. And in relationship, real relationship, the romantic blinders can cause problems. Maybe I have a problem.

That's why Rebekah Freedom's article from the *Elephant Journal*, "Loving the Person & Not the Potential," spoke to me so clearly. Each line is a deeper stage of awareness, for me.

Love your time and be aware how you spend it.

I absolutely love being in love. I love the feeling of intoxication. I will even over-create that feeling to unlock the muse. And occasionally the illusion is all mine and terrifying to the object of desire. Okay.

Love your body and be aware how you use it.

Oh sex. Oh how loving another body begins to shine up my

own image of my body. How being in relationship to another and receiving gifts and appreciations of skin time give so much energy and momentum to my life. Hmm. Does this mean I'm addicted? How can I bring this sense of self-love inside?

Love your thoughts and be aware how you focus them.

I do love the thoughts generated by this intoxicating reverie. And I can get lost in the feelings so far that I lose perspective to see the other parts of a relationship. I can over-love and thus overlook things that are not working, In the case of my marriage, I can love-through things that were broken and somehow believe that it was still some form of bliss. It was not. It was sublimation of love in order to hold on to the illusion that love was still present.

Love your feelings and how they move you.

I am learning better how to tap into the power of feelings and how they can motivate me towards doing better, being better. But I'm also too aware of how my feelings can lead me down dark and lonely paths. I am constantly trying to find the balanced walk down the middle.

The only way I've learned to keep the balance in real life is to focus on the present moment. The skin in front of me. The kiss that is presented in real life. And the body that I have at this very moment, loveable and true. It's a hard exercise, and I often don't live up to it. But I do understand that I am creating this love blitz. I can choose to create it and not to share it directly with the engine of my desire, my partner, my date, my lover. I don't have to share everything.

Breathe in, breathe out. Enjoy this moment. Write about its

potential if you want, go with the flow, capture the deepest love or deepest pain you can reach, and then return to the present. Like a meditation. It's only a thought, let it go. Breathe. It's only a feeling, return to the breath.

Ah. That's the idea.

*Source: Rebekah Freedom, "Loving the Person & Not the Potential," *Elephant Journal*, May 2014.

46.

We Have So Few Chances to Feel Loved

This is about my family of origin and my willingness to try and outgrow, out-love, out-inspire some deep wounding in the other person. I don't look for wounded people, but when I find them, I should run for the hills. I need a whole person for my whole person.

I don't know what I need. I don't know what kind of woman, or what a healthy relationship really looks like. I mean, I've read books. I've imagined. I've written posts and poetry about it until I've created my own surreal ideal. But I am clear, I have no idea what I'm talking about.

And since my divorce, I've had ONE connection. A few relationships, but one connection that lifted all of my hopes and ideas. And from this wonderful infusion of energy and hope I constructed pyramids and offerings to the gods of love. Because there was something, some little glimmer, that really turned me on about this woman.

I guess I can say this now, because it's gone. Her fears and objections finally won out over my optimism, regeneration, and attempts to repair the breakups that kept happening. Okay, so that was a clue that something was not right between us. And the further I launched into "being okay" with her constantly not being okay, the more I moved away from my core truth. The flow has to go both ways.

How did I get fooled into thinking a woman who had done

very little "work" on herself post-divorce was going to heal in my light of love? What a crock. The work ahead for her is for herself alone. And unfortunately, now we both get to move on alone and heal without the rubbing and joy that our "relationship" was causing. The joy was apparent in both of us. The chemistry was hot. The sex... Well, I'll use discretion and not talk about that.

Coming out of a failed marriage, both partners often feel damaged and depressed. In my case, I was certain that I would never love again. Of course, that was my depression talking, but when you are Sad, you can get pretty dark. So there's this concept, from a divorce recovery class I took, called the Healing Relationship.

I was determined not to be this woman's healing relationship. And I worked hard to make myself as flexible as possible. To recede when she needed space. To not share the poems and inspirations I was feeling about her, so that she wouldn't get freaked out.

But you see, the freak-out was the problem. And I was not going to be able to fix it, no matter what I did, or how well I behaved. There would simply be another freak-out, regardless of how it started, and we would hit the rocks.

During my failing marriage, I got very good at listening for the sirens of destruction (I had done something wrong) and looking for escape or some heroic journey to fix the problem. Both in my marriage and in this relationship, that was not the right approach. But I didn't want to accept the warning signs I was being hit over the head with. I didn't want to accept defeat in my marriage, and in some microcosm of the same role-relationship, I didn't want to accept that this woman I was "crazy about" was going to toss me out because she was afraid.

Again, it was more than her fear. It was everything.

She was hungry for affection and love. But she recoiled from what she needed soon after she began getting it. She was overly protective of her son, but that's what single moms do. She is still deeply angry at her ex and continuously upset by the dickish-ex he has become. And for sure, he is a dick, both to her and their son. He has no excuse.

On the other hand, she has no excuse either. And actually, I have no excuse. I have no excuse for continuing a relationship that I could see was full of "holy shit, what's wrong now" moments. But the chemistry was on. And I had not felt chemistry for a long, long time. I might be addicted to hot chemistry, or sex, but not getting either for years and years was a harsh form of torture for someone like me who thrives on touch.

And we touched, but she pushed me off sometimes. And she told me constantly how we would eventually break up, and she mused occasionally about what it would be that would finally do it.

I must've learned in my family of origin, as a little boy, how to repair and attempt resuscitation for bad relationships. I tried and tried to keep my parents together. I excelled at school. I excelled in football and tennis. I was a childhood magician. I worked hard as the mascot or hero child to keep everyone happy. And when my parents split for the first time, because of my dad's drinking, I was the one who brought them back together.

I'm not making this up. That's what I was told, by my alcoholic father. And when the "try" didn't work and my mom left for Mexico with everyone but me and my dad, I again went into hyper-performance mode to try to make things better. But there was no fixing my dad. Over the next two years he fought to win me. I think it was more about the money than me, but he liked to tell me he was doing it for me. Of course, he was drunk when he was telling me this, but that didn't keep it from registering deeply in my 7-year-old heart.

I can't repair a broken person. No one can. And my first "love" post-divorce was no different. And even as I bucked against the breakups and saw the signs that this was a deeply wounded person, I was addicted to the... what?

Was I enjoying the suffering? I don't think so. Was it familiar? Very. Did the dramatic breakups feel familiar? Yep, right out of the last four years of my marriage.

But she would not be healed by me or anyone else. She would only recover from her anger and sadness about her divorce by going through it, in some sort of therapeutic setting. And I was not that path. I didn't fantasize that I was the healer, but I DID try to be big enough to contain her thrashing against the feelings towards and against me. These feelings were more about her and her ex than anything I brought to the relationship. It's sad to see it happening. And I was soooooo connected to her physically. But of course, that's my obsession.

Well, ultimately the book of poems wasn't enough. Even with the crowning poem being a direct plea to her, or protestation, or warning... it's hard to tell sometimes. But the poems were definitely me expressing MY wants and HOPES regardless of what I was seeing in her actions.

In recovery of any kind, it is not for us to fix each other. The support is so we can find our own path to fixing ourselves. And as we find ourselves in relationships with unhealthy people, it is our responsibility to do what is best for our health. And trying to be supportive and loving is one of those things we can do. Trying to be loving enough to get them to change, well, that's the trap right there.

So I wanted to change her. No doubt about it. I could say it with a straight face, full-well knowing that I was nuts. I wanted to blow her wide open with stability and love poems and clarity of intention. But... as the story goes, every. single. time. there is no fixing the other person. And the more we work towards or wait for them to change, the further we get from our own integrity.

At the core, my healing is at stake with the breakup of this relationship. I felt deeply for the first time since my divorce. I had moments of hope, "Wow, this is amazing, she is amazing, we could be amazing." And then the red flag, more like a red bazooka, would blow a hole in my theory of love in the time of recovery.

For people to be loved, they have to love themselves. And that loving cannot come in the form of caring for another person (a child, for example) or by going through it while IN a relationship. No, in my understanding of recovery, in general, the recovery has to take place in the individual, regardless of the support or lack of support in the person's surroundings.

There was simply no way I could love this woman enough. She was not mine to fix. And I knew this. I still know this. But the pain of losing a "loving feeling" is also hard. I would've continued to heal, retry, reset, over and over to keep the physical connection. But I was covering up the disconnection that had nothing to do with me. I wanted to be loved. I wanted things to be ecstatic. And I was willing to toss my own instincts and knowledge down the tube for a while in order to feel or not feel this sense of being loved.

I don't believe we have a soul mate. I believe we have connections. And for me, a connection requires chemistry. But the chemistry, while essential to the growth of a real relationship, is only a small portion of what is required to develop a relationship. And that's really what I want. I want a relationship. I don't want a recovery project. I don't want to fix someone. I want her to come to me healthy, happy, energetic, and done with a good portion of their baggage.

Well, that's not who struck my heart with a warm glow. But that's whom I now recover from myself, as I return to working my own issues out, again. I have to walk away from my own issues in this relationship, in hopes of being a whole and ready man when the next potential shows up.

47.

Present and Future Planning in Your Relationship

We've all got stress. We've all got moments, Friday afternoons are a great example, when the breaking point is reached, and if we're lucky, the weekend is ready to open up before us. Ah, the WEEKEND. A time to cut loose, rest, rebuild ourselves and our love lives, and… And then we still find time and need to be distracted. Taken off point. Unplugged from our goals, plans, work, whatever.

I pull my headphones on, engage the noise-canceling function, and boom, I'm in a moment of zen, right in my living room. Turns out, sometimes I'm just looking to be distracted. Even the good things (okay, the great things) are often stressful.

There had been too many good things to even list. But I still needed time to disconnect. I guess we call it "alone time," but sometimes it is just isolation time for me.

Isolation is a funny thing. I can be Facebooking like mad, reading five articles on five tabs in my browser and taking notes for new post, and I feel like I'm really connected, alive, multitasking. But, if I'm honest, I can see how my social media passion is also an escape from the present.

I first encountered the concepts of backwards and forwards time in *Time and the Art of Living* by Robert Grudin. Here's my basic paraphrase.

> 1. Present Moment. What we're all striving to stay focused on. Meditation. Awareness. Conscious sex. Honest conversations. Listening. Hitting flow. Whatever you want to call it.
>
> 2. Thoughts about the future.
>
> 3. Memories of the past.

Although I do think that keeping our attention on the present moment is a very powerful tool, at times these two other modes of time can be helpful and illuminating as well.

Projecting ourselves into the future can be a wonderful exercise. We can begin to set goals and ideas for what we want, what we are looking forward to in the new experience. Setting up a framework for the future plans. And sometimes the projections in themselves can be lovely moments.

I was buying a new house. She said, "We can have romantic evenings in front of the fireplace." And of course, we will. But in this very moment, projecting our ideas, we could go there together. And everything, absolutely everything could be perfect in our minds. This positive projecting can have bonding and energizing effects on us. We can find motivation and inspiration for what needs to be done to create the perfect moment we visualized.

It's not as if the longing for that future moment causes us to miss out on some experience of the present moment. Actually, in projecting ourselves into this future-perfect moment we are creating an image of reality that we can actively create. (Did I get too woowoo on you there?) Let me give you a quote from Grudin's book.

> Fast drivers can see no further than slow drivers, but they must look further down the road to time their reactions safely. Similarly, people with great projects afoot habitually look further and more clearly into the future than people who are mired in day-to-day concerns. These former control the future because by necessity they must project themselves into it; and the upshot is, that like ambitions settlers, they stake out larger plots and homesteads of time than the rest of us. The do not easily grow sad or old; they are seldom intimidated by the alarms and confusions of the present because they have something greater of their own, some sense of their large and coherent motion in time, to compare the present with. – *Robert Grudin*

So projection of a great project means together we can map out some ideas about what we want to create, not just physically, but emotionally as well.

A relationship is a lot like this. You state ideas and dreams to see if the other person resonates and lights up. Like a trial balloon.

"Wow, this cold night feels like New York City," I said once.

"Do you want to go to New York City together?" she asked, clutching my arm against the wind and splinters of mist.

"Yes, that would be awesome. To walk the streets together. Like this."

And with that she took several steps over the next week to book a trip together. This was still pretty early on in our relationship. WOW. I remember thinking, "What the heck? New York, so soon?" And what I learned was that she likes to set plans in motion, she likes to have events or travels to look forward to.

Almost like my big ideas that pull me along. She has a different type of creativity. Hers is for dreaming up what's next and then making the dream a reality.

Present moment work helps us stay focused on our jobs, our projects, and kids. Yet we can take wild flights of fancy into our imaginary future relationship as we give voice to various whimsical and fantastical ideas.

Stay focused in the present moment but do allow yourself to dream and project into the future with your partner. Opening those doors of dreaming together can be a gateway of power.

48.

The Three Essential Elements of Love

It is easier to say what didn't work than to count up the things that did work. Especially as we arrive at the end of yet another relationship (dating, marriage), it is more common to identify the things that broke down. But in focusing on the positive aspects of what has worked in the past, you might be able to focus your attention there. Looking for the positive as opposed to looking out to avoid the negative.

Here are the three essential elements of love, in my experience thus far:

1. Joy

2. Calm center

3. Passion

There you go, those are the keys to love. Let's take them one by one and see if we can illuminate what makes love blossom in the company of someone with these qualities.

Joy

You know it when you feel it, and you recognize it when you see it in another person. There is no faking inner joy. Positivism can help, but the peaks and valleys of life puncture positivism all the time. The joyous person stumbles just like the rest of us but tends to get back up quicker and with a hopefulness that accelerates the recovery.

We are all looking for joy, both in our lives and in the relationship with another person. If there is a huge imbalance in the levels of innate joy, trouble lies ahead. And maybe there are highly joyous people and people who are comfortable and fine in a more medium joyousness. Perhaps I am asking for someone to match my highly activated happiness. And maybe it's more important to understand your own energy and set-point of joy, as then you can align yourself with a similar inner smile.

What demonstrates joy? How do we recognize this joyousness?

Smiles that light up the eyes are a good start. Even from a distance, if you are tuned in, you can feel a joyous person enter a restaurant. It's an amazing recognition. And when you see it, feel it, taste the hint of joy in the other person, you can no longer do without it. I remember standing next to a date at an art reception and being rather painfully aware of her self-consciousness and overthinking, while being a bit blown over by a woman, several groups of people over, whom I recognized as a fellow radiator.

Perhaps not everyone radiates at the same intensity. If you are a highly joyous person, like myself, perhaps anything less will be painful and disconnecting. I know that I seek joy above all else in my next relationship. I will settle for nothing less.

Calm center

With all the tumbles in life, we all deal with setbacks and interruptions in our own ways. If there is drama in our lives, we can either respond with more drama or urgency, or we can pause and re-evaluate. I am a slow down and observe what's going on type. When the drama hits from outside my life, I do my best not to respond in kind with more drama. I have always scored very low on the "sense of urgency" scale. It's one of the things, I think, that drove my then-wife crazy. She always felt she was the only one responding with the appropriate action.

But I'm not looking for any more drama or urgency in my life. The world brings out enough of that in our lives without us contributing to the frenetic pace. Calm centering is one of my super powers.

If your partner is also a centering person, you might have a better chance at finding that inner peace together, in spite of the drama around you. Listen to their words. Listen to how they express the frustrations of the day. You want to hear a lack of victimization. You want to hear a simple pragmatic approach to getting the tasks and chores of life accomplished without struggle. Sometimes there will be frustration and energy, that's okay. But what is not okay is the needless amplification of the urgency of any issue.

"Is someone going to the hospital?" If the answer is no, then you can take your time in the response. And, especially in dealing with your ex-partner, the pause is your friend. They no longer respond within minutes, they no longer have to. So you too have the option to wait a bit before responding to any request. Time is on your side. Not manipulative time, but time to pause, reset, think, and respond.

It is always a good idea to get your center before responding to a dramatic or urgent message. Again, unless there is a fire or someone needs to go to the hospital, the urgency is probably falsely constructed to elicit a response. Give your response, on your time, by taking a moment to breathe and think about what you want as a result.

Passion

What keeps you up at night? How are you envisioning your life beyond the daily grind? Do you have goals that transcend your role as a parent or worker bee? If you don't, this might be a good time to figure out what other goals you can put out there for yourself. You need bigger goals. Call them life work, hobbies, or passions. You need to have some bigger ideals and bigger visions for your own life.

Seeing that passion in another person may be the final critical element I look for. I want a passionate partner. I want to be a cheerleader for your dreams. Of course I am sensitive to your needs and goals for your kids, but I'm most interested in what warms your synapses in the off times.

Tell me about your dreams. What are you passionate about?

I have a few things that I will slowly reveal to you as well, as we get to know each other. But I don't want to overwhelm you. I don't want to brag or show off with what I'm working towards. But it's one of my most prized accomplishments. Sure, I love my kids. And I am clear that they are the priority in my life, way beyond my ultimate dreams for myself. BUT... they will grow older and no longer require my utmost attention and nurture. What will I be doing after they are gone?

Retirement is not an option for me. The time gained in divorce has been a boon to my big dreams. (My blog and then this book, for example, are a direct result of having the additional time when I don't have my kids.) So as I continue to move through my life, I am growing my bigger dream. I am gathering momentum as an artist, writer, musician, and poet. I am happy with my alone time. I would love to have you alongside me, grooving to your own dream. And together we can bond and thrive in support of our mutual time together and our individual dreams.

I'm almost always hopeful and joyous about this new journey. As a single dad, I have more time and more complications than when I was married. And if we can find the balance of these three traits between us, perhaps we can build "what's next" together.

I'm looking for a together partner, and a partner who is together already.

49.

Fierce Love - What You're Looking for

Love is complex, and relationships are a disaster, unless you find someone who can mirror back some of your favorite qualities. What I am looking for in my next relationship is **fierce love**. A love that never gives up. NO. MATTER. WHAT.

When you find it you will know. The other person will have a tenacity, a desire to BE IN A RELATIONSHIP, and one that will last.

Sure, the initial bliss cannot last. After six months or so the burning desire is fulfilled and you settle into something more realistic, more like real life.

But imagine being in a relationship with another person who is going to fight to keep the relationship healthy and moving forward. Imagine.

Nothing is easy in relationships. After the honeymoon phase, the mundane sets in, and that's where you get your real tests. You take each other for granted. You do things that piss off the other person. You have to compromise in ways you had forgotten were necessary during your "single" period.

Fierce love says, no matter what, I'm IN. I've done this before, I know what I'm looking for, and you're it. But you've got to let me know you're in it for the long haul as well.

And we should both be fighters. Imagine our optimism when we're both fierce about fighting for our relationship to work. Sure, we go through rough patches, a disagreement, an angry word, but we come back stronger and more committed each time. There is no growth without risk. And if you have the risk of your relationship covered up, you can grow and expand the boundaries for both of you.

That's what we want. Ascendant love. Moving ever higher together. Fearlessly attacking the discord as it arrives unwelcome and unbidden. And we move through it with the other person, knowing that person is going to stick around.

Be fierce in your love and fierce in your anger. They are two sides of the same coin. And when you are committed, the fierceness becomes the glue that keeps your relationship together.

Sure, we'll have challenges tomorrow. And we'll procrastinate and avoid for a little while, but we'll come back together with a fire and rage that says, "You're mine."

Fierce is good. If love is what you're looking for, look for people with fierceness in their eyes. Always.

50.

The Spiritual Quest for Love

> On the spiritual path, there's nothing to get, and everything to get rid of. ... The first thing to let go of is trying to get love, and instead to give it. That's the secret of the spiritual path.
>
> – Ayya Khema, "What Love Is"

In the company of friends, I talk a lot about how I met my last partner. We both talked about how "the time was right" for both of us. And how "the stars or gods aligned in our favor." And to be sure, we are both very prayerful and thankful people. And each morning when we woke up together, there was a lot of gratitude between us, for us, about us. But another element came first that bonded us in a way that no previous relationship or marriage had done before, for either of us.

Spiritual and kinda religious

When you are alone, everything in your world is colored by your own internal thoughts and feelings. And your strategies and prayers are your own alone. When you join with another person, your songs and prayers add a "together" element that I believe is transformative.

Seeking, longing, looking for love

When there is an absence of love in your life, for many of us, it is like a missing piece of our soul. The term "empath" has been getting a lot of play lately, in describing people who feel into others empathetically. And what I'm well aware of about myself is that, in the absence of a love relationship, my experience of joy, passion, and elation is greatly diminished. I glow more brightly when I have another person to resonate with. So in my seeking, post-divorce, I have been looking for a resonance in both physical and spiritual terms.

So you set out on your noble quest to find a new relationship. In my case I set up profiles on a few of the online dating sites. eHarmony: nope, give me the ability to browse people, don't tell me who you think I match with. Match.com: a bit better, larger audience, fairly interesting profiles, and you pay, so you're looking for something. OkCupid – my favorite site, because of the random and often revealing questions, it's free, but it has a lot of people who are just playing around, not looking for a relationship.

And for the record, I had a few dates via Match and OkCupid that were interesting. I learned several things about myself in my first rush at "getting back in the game."

- I was not interested in casual sex.
- I was not able to feign interest when the person was boring.
- A lot of profiles (pictures and stories) are outright fabrications.
- A lot of people are playing on dating sites but have no intention of dating.

The Spiritual Quest for Love 243

I had some interesting insights in filling out my several profiles. Eventually I hit on one that seemed to attract the right mix of women. Interest in a long-term relationship and actively pursuing their own dream, project, agenda. I was clear, I was not interested in "dating." Dating to me means several things:

- Actively in pursuit
- Not looking for commitment
- More interested in entertainment
- Drinking was part of the focus for 90% of the daters.
- Interested in lots of dates, lots of entertainment, maybe playing the field

The first real relationship I had was from Match.com. The first contact was from her to me. (Very rare.) When I was non-responsive, she followed up with a second email that said, "Hey, I was looking at your profile wondering why I we hadn't gone out on a date yet and then I realized, hey, this guy didn't respond to my email. So I thought I'd ask, 'What's the deal? Is there something wrong with my picture or profile?'"

And this first relationship changed everything and eventually set me up for success later down the path. Girlfriend 1 was a tiny bit older, wiser, and a few more years down the road of the post-divorce routine. But most importantly, she shared the same love language: touch. BOOM, a light went off during our first week together.

In two marriages combining into 17 years, I had never felt as adored and loved as I did with this woman. She easily engaged in hugging, holding hands, and other physical signs of affection. And just like me, she reach out for that touch *all the time.* And she was also comfortable expressing her affection verbally. She would just tell me, "You are so damn cute." Like, out of the blue. And every time I heard it, I was surprised. "Me?" And the real surprising part was how infrequently I heard that during the entire course of my two marriages. Touch is language number one, but words of affection also play a strong role in my constellation of what "feels like love."

The nearest miss

This first relationship was missing one ingredient for me, something that didn't immediately click. But since we had both been through a divorce recovery class, we had a label for what had happened. She even predicted this outcome in that first amazing week at the beginning.

"I may be the healing relationship for you, and that's okay," she said. "I've had mine, and I know what I'm looking for. And I'm okay if this is just a crush. Let's see where things go and not get too far ahead of just being together."

She was right. As I reignited with the proximity of her physical affection and began to find my inner joy again, I began to look beyond the present moment and into what relationship goals I had, beyond her. In the moments between Christmas and New Year's Day, we found the space to separate without a whimper. We both knew it wasn't The One. And we were both committed to finding The One. And with that, we also wanted the other person to have the best relationship. We had breakfast the morning after we "broke up." I remember a few tiny tears but mainly the big realization at how much I loved her. And when the romantic relationship was out of the way, I could fully feel my adoration of her. We're still friends, confidants, and virtual wingmen, as we encourage each other, even now, to get what we really want.

Reset and rebuild

I went through a year after breaking up with her before I ran into my next girlfriend. The year in the middle involved a lot of rebuilding and remembering what made me happy. On that back porch, Girlfriend 1 asked me, obviously aware that I was struggling a bit, "What do you look like when you are happy? What kinds of things do you do?" Those two sentences became my mantra over the next year. I hit the online sites again and went out on a few dates, with no real connections. And repeatedly learned that an evening drinking a glass of wine with someone who wasn't even a near miss was a true waste of an evening. I slowed down my efforts to find my next date.

I started looking at what things made me happy. I reconnected with my music and started looking for musicians to play with again. I started attending a tennis workout several times a week. I started a focused walking program in the foothills around my house. I was building the new me. I was determined to become the happy me, the one who would attract the next girlfriend rather than have to go out advertising myself on Match.com.

As I was starting to "feel my oats" in spite of some financial setbacks I crossed paths with my next girlfriend: the tennis player. We flamed up and flamed out fairly quickly, but she also taught me a few valuable lessons.

With Girlfriend 2 we had the physical spark that had been missing in my first relationship. And we had tennis. That was enough to keep a lopsided relationship going for a good bit of the summer. But something was amiss. And this time it was easier to pull back when the signs became more obvious that the "relationship" was something I wanted but she didn't. I was willing to create 90% of the connection in order to keep playing tennis and keep up the illusion that we were building a relationship.

We were not building a relationship. And when I was able to see this, I was also able to say goodbye without anger and to affirm my ability to break up well.

The turning point

This second relationship showed me what was missing from the first relationship and showed me my own blind side of being the overachieving optimist. I was willing to overlook the dysfunction in the name of relationship. But that's not how it's supposed to go. And I knew it wasn't working out, but I continued a few more cycles of passion-breakup-passion-breakup before I opted out.

And at this point I made a fundamental shift. I was going to take my dating profiles down. I was going to work exclusively on my own program of becoming a better tennis player, a better and more confident musician, and a more confident me. I made a fundamental shift away from pursuit and back towards self-work.

My idea was, I wanted to become the person she would fall in love with. I even wrote a poem to her, before I had any concept of her, almost as a prayer.

The spiritual message:
The first thing to let go of is trying to get love, and instead to give it.

That's the moment we began reframing out future ideas while including some other person in the picture. I began writing constantly about not dating and going offline and real time instead. I also had been writing almost daily love poems. The poems of desire, I called them. But they were also like a call for someone to answer. Like this fragment from "burning up in prayer":

> she's probably here
> in the organic grocery store
> if i could just send up a flag
> rebroadcast my tinder beacon
> if she were receiving my vibe
> indications are that she is not
> but i search amidst the kale
> and organic bubble bath

Timing is everything.

So, is it timing or god that brings us together at the perfect moment? I don't know the answer to that, but I do know this: someone can walk into your life and change everything you've ever wanted or imagined you wanted. When that happens, you are either prepared for departure and flight, or you are not.

There is growth and adventure ahead. Prayerful thanksgiving throughout our daily lives merely affirms what we feel and hope. The path may be winding and long, but here are the basics.

1. Learn what you really need in your relationship.

2. Learn what you must jettison from any future relationship.

3. Keep focused on your own life, your own growth, your ripeness.

4. When the moment arrives, be fearless in your commitment to love fully.

5. Stay in the present moment.

6. Listen for and discuss issues as they arise.

7. Celebrate the spiritual and physical connections in your life together.

8. Press ever onward and upward together – limitless.

Any divergence from this path is a distraction. If you want the relationship you've hungered for, settling for anything less may teach you some valuable lessons, but you eventually have to move on.

I want a relationship. I don't want to spend time "dating" or trying to impress someone. I want a woman to show up in my life fully formed, fully empowered, and fully ready to take off with me. I am prepared to give myself in the same way.

www.ingramcontent.com/pod-product-compliance
Lightning Source LLC
Chambersburg PA
CBHW050532300426
44113CB00012B/2051